HEALTHCARE PHILANTHROPY

Betsy Chapin Taylor

HEALTHCARE PHILANTHROPY

ADVANCE CHARITABLE GIVING TO YOUR ORGANIZATION'S MISSION

ACHE Management Series

ASSOCIATION FOR
HEALTHCARE
PHILANTHROPY℠

Connecting People • Enriching Lives

Library of Congress Cataloging-in-Publication Data
Taylor, Betsy Chapin.
   Healthcare philanthropy : advance charitable giving to your organization's mission / Betsy Chapin Taylor.
      p. cm.
   Includes bibliographical references and index.
   ISBN 978-1-56793-449-6 (alk. paper)
  1. Hospitals–Endowments. 2. Hospitals–Finance. 3. Fund raising. 4. Hospitals–United States. I. Title.
   RA971.3.T39 2012
   362.11068'1–dc23
                              2012017250

The paper used in this publication meets the minimum requirements of American National Standard for Information Sciences—Permanence of Paper for Printed Library Materials, ANSI Z39.48-1984. ♾™

Acquisitions editor: Janet Davis; Project manager: Jennifer Seibert; Cover designer: Anne LoCascio; Layout: Fine Print, Ltd.

Found an error or a typo? We want to know! Please e-mail it to hap1@ache.org, and put "Book Error" in the subject line.

For photocopying and copyright information, please contact Copyright Clearance Center at www.copyright.com or at (978) 750–8400.

   Health Administration Press
   A division of the Foundation of the American
      College of Healthcare Executives
   One North Franklin Street, Suite 1700
   Chicago, IL 60606–3529
   (312) 424–2800

*This book is dedicated
with love and gratitude to*

*My mother,
Linda Standefer Chapin.
She was a gracious force for good,
a tireless advocate for the noble work of philanthropy,
a wise and gentle leader,
and my greatest friend.*

*And my father,
Edward Young Chapin IV.
He quietly gave much to help many,
believed even when I didn't,
loved me unconditionally,
and was my tireless encourager.*

Their impact continues on in the many lives they touched.

Contents

Foreword

At the 2011 international conference of the Association for Healthcare Philanthropy (AHP), my colleagues and I had the pleasure of presenting a Fellow certification medallion to Betsy Chapin Taylor, who has been a member of AHP since 1995. This credential, based on knowledge, testing, and achievement in the field of healthcare philanthropy, is AHP's highest recognition. In Betsy Chapin Taylor's case, earning this certification demonstrates her profound sense of dedication to advancing our profession.

Betsy brings to her outstanding work as a development professional a prolific and diverse academic and career background. It is, therefore, no surprise that she has produced an extremely informative, well-organized, well-written book in which she shares her expertise, addressing head-on and in plain, highly effective language that which those who serve healthcare organizations in a range of leadership and clinical positions need to know and need to do to advance charitable giving. Drawing on a wide array of studies, interviews with practitioners, and a refreshing dose of common sense, she introduces and builds concepts central to fostering and maintaining viable and productive philanthropic programs capable of providing significant, reliable support to healthcare institutions.

The clarity with which she presents the importance of the CEO's leadership in healthcare philanthropy and the essential elements of the involvement and participation of physicians, board members, and donors are evidence enough of Betsy's understanding of what is required to grow philanthropy in healthcare institutions. These insights do much to assist in bringing philanthropy to a meaningful and heightened level of importance for new impact in hospitals and all healthcare organizations.

The underlying dynamic Betsy emphasizes is the cultivation of relationships. From the outset, she emphasizes attributes that distinguish *philanthropy*—"a mutually rewarding and genuine partnership"—from *fundraising*, which she describes as "transactional and reactive" and characterized by "little depth or richness to the relationship between the donor and the organization." With this important distinction in mind, she illustrates the interactive network of roles for healthcare executives, board members, physicians, development officers, and staff as they relate to one another and to donors, patients, and the larger community.

Healthcare Philanthropy: Advance Charitable Giving to Your Organization's Mission presents a clear vision of what it means to create a culture of philanthropy and provides sage advice about how to instill that vision throughout the institution. This is a must-read book for every C-suite executive and board member.

William C. McGinly, PhD, CAE
President, Chief Executive Officer
Association for Healthcare Philanthropy

Preface

THIS BOOK WAS written for healthcare CEOs, other senior executives, and board members who wish to create a philanthropy program or enhance an existing one to harness the power of voluntary charitable giving in advancing a healthcare organization's healing mission.

An organization's leaders and board have considerable power to elevate philanthropy on the agenda. This book provides these most important allies with the context and tools they need to build a dependable and successful philanthropy program. It explores the rationale for positioning philanthropy as a vital revenue source, identifies high-impact roles and responsibilities for strategic partners, and delves into key levers organizations can deploy to strengthen philanthropy programs. Each chapter also includes a list of specific actions that will help organizations optimize performance.

Ultimately, this book aims to enable vibrant and mutually rewarding partnerships with donors that add genuine value to the healthcare organization and all those it serves.

Betsy Chapin Taylor
Chattanooga, Tennessee
February 2012

Acknowledgments

THERE IS NO way to adequately recognize all those who have touched this book or encouraged me. So, with hopes for forgiveness for the generalizations, here are some of the many people who deserve to be acknowledged:

Donors, board members, healthcare executives, and foundation colleagues—It has been a privilege to work alongside you to bring health and hope to communities.

The philanthropy leaders who generously contributed interviews and resources to the book and made it so much richer and more resonant—You have all inspired me.

The amazing professionals at Health Administration Press who nurtured this book in countless ways, including Eileen Lynch, who helped start this process; acquisitions editor Janet Davis, who skillfully kept everything running in an orderly fashion; editor Jen Seibert, whose thoughtful editing added immense value while making the process downright fun; assistant director Michael Cunningham, who deftly finessed the details; and vice president Maureen Glass, for her valued support.

Bill McGinly, Kathy Renzetti, and Monika Schulz of the Association for Healthcare Philanthropy, for championing a meaningful partnership for this book with an organization that has given me both roots and wings in this profession.

My valued colleagues at the American College of Healthcare Executives—I'm proud to be part of your superior work. Special thanks to Howard Horwitz for letting me be part of his team and to Jennifer Manthei for making time on the road well-orchestrated and fun.

My dear friends and esteemed mentors, but especially Paige Stowell, Jean Landmesser, Brenda Grant, Emilia Pastina Jones, Dotty Allen, Ann Thompson-Haas, Kay Sprinkel Grace, and Dr. Christine Riordan.

Most of all, thanks to my precious family. My husband, Brent, and daughters, Grace and Elise, not only spent Saturdays without me while I wrote but also are the greatest joy in my life. Dad was my tireless cheerleader and asked about the book even in our very last conversation. Mom was the angel on my shoulder guiding every page. Ted and John are not only great brothers but also great friends.

Thanks and immense gratitude to each of you.

Betsy

PART I

Introduction

CHAPTER 1

The Rationale for Philanthropy

We move from an era in which philanthropy
was icing on the cake to one in which
philanthropy is an essential ingredient.

—*Healthcare Financial Management Association*

IN THE DARK skies of financial challenge that have been brewing over healthcare for some time, a menacing thundercloud has emerged. American healthcare organizations face a range of revenue issues, including tightening reimbursement from all payers, declining volumes, lower-paying observation days once considered inpatient days, heavily audited claims, a rise in high-deductible insurance, and the implementation of healthcare reform. The sustainable capital investment threshold for healthcare recommended by Moody's Investors Service (2006)—a 5 percent operating margin—is elusive for most organizations and impossible for many. Furthermore, many organizations have achieved stronger bottom lines in recent years only because of staffing reductions and supply cuts that are likely unsustainable (Shinkman 2010).

Industry news reflects the difficulties of obtaining capital to fuel investment:

- Seventy-seven percent of healthcare CEOs name financial challenges as their top concern—the sixth year in a row financial constraints have topped the list in an annual CEO survey by the American College of Healthcare Executives (2011).

- Hospital operating margins continue to hover around 2 percent, well below the 5 percent recommended for sustainable capital reinvestment (Moody's Investors Service 2010).
- This decade, healthcare reform will reduce Medicare and Medicaid payments, which account for more than half of hospital revenues, by $155 billion. While charity care loads will allegedly ease when coverage expands in 2014, hospitals will still need to achieve tremendous growth to compensate for cuts (Gearon 2011).
- Hospital bond rating downgrades will "likely increase in the short term unless expense reductions and productivity gains compensate for stagnant or weak revenue growth" (Goldstein 2011).

Added to these challenges are the ambiguity of healthcare reform and its undefined infrastructure. Reform has been described as "even more mysterious than unicorns. No one has seen either one, but at least we know what a unicorn looks like" (Nocera 2011). *US News & World Report* shares some of the tensions at issue: "Imagine running a heavily regulated business where the pressure is on improving the quality of your service while lowering prices, but your largest payers don't even cover your costs—and they promise to pinch you even more. Add to the mix the overwhelming pressure to change your entire business model, even though it doesn't make financial sense to do so today" (Gearon 2011). Significant healthcare legislation in the past, such as Medicaid and Medicare, has gone through many iterations and revisions, so the eventual impact of healthcare reform is unclear. However, this ambiguity does not remove the need to prepare for what indications point to: further erosion of operating profitability.

While hospitals' ability to access capital is constrained, halting continued investment in the organization is not an option. The need for capital investment is unrelenting as hospitals work to renovate and replace deteriorating physical plants, keep up with the brisk pace of clinical innovation, implement sweeping information technology initiatives, and advance other valuable projects—all of which compete for limited capital. They are also under pressure to grow and maintain competitive market position, capture new opportunities, meet state and federal mandates, and simply ward off obsolescence. Furthermore, some projects cannot be delayed even though they do not bring a direct financial return.

In short, the menacing thundercloud is the stuff of sleepless nights for CEOs, senior executives, and boards trying to navigate an increasingly complex environment. Healthcare organizations are unlikely to discover a quick fix for declining revenues, and while they are working hard to allocate resources wisely, they may reach a point where they do not have enough to accomplish the basics, much less fulfill their aspirations for long-term growth and profitability.

THE PROMISE OF PHILANTHROPY

Healthcare organizations have traditionally relied on three key strategies for obtaining critical dollars to sustain and strengthen their efforts:

- Revenue from operations and investments
- Debt
- Sale of assets

Organizations have also set aside money to finance capital expenditures through funded depreciation. Some safety net providers also have disproportionate share payments or other forms of offsets.

For most healthcare organizations, these traditional funding sources are no longer adequate to meet escalating capital needs, and the cost and difficulty of using debt to fund future plans have increased. Left with few unneeded, saleable assets, healthcare organizations have to seek other revenue opportunities. A silver lining offers promise in the form of a largely underutilized source of revenue: voluntary charitable giving, also known as *philanthropy*. Philanthropy has emerged as a viable option for a variety of reasons, and now is the time to advance this strategy to achieve maximum impact.

A Return to Our Roots

American healthcare was founded on a tradition of voluntary giving to advance the greater good, so turning to philanthropy is returning to our roots.

The American inclination to give emerged as early as 1630, when Puritan John Winthrop shared his sermon "A Model on Christian Charity" with pilgrims preparing to board the ship *Arbella* to come to this new nation. In this sermon, Winthrop laid out an expectation that those settling in the new land create a "city on a hill"—a community model of social responsibility (Bremer 2009).

By 1710, preacher Cotton Mather was concerned that the zeal for upholding the ideals of social obligation was waning, so he published a directive called *Essays to Do Good* to stoke the fires of the nation's hearts. He reminded the young nation that "a power and an opportunity to do good, not only gives a right to the doing of it, but makes the doing of it a duty" and called for improving the nation's social fabric through such deeds as founding hospitals to advance the public good (Mather 1816).

Benjamin Franklin, who was influenced by the teachings of Winthrop and Mather, was the first to position healthcare philanthropy as a civic responsibility. Franklin's friend, surgeon Dr. Thomas Bond, proposed the idea of founding a hospital that served both the sick and the mentally ill of Philadelphia, with a focus on alleviating the suffering of the poor. When Bond's initial efforts to raise charitable funds for this purpose floundered, Franklin helped establish a hospital board in 1752 to lead the charge. Trustees were chosen on the basis of personal wealth and civic connections because they had the most potential to foster charitable support.

Franklin gathered men from across Philadelphia to share the vision and ask for charitable investment. Subscribing to some of the same ideas about charity still used in capital campaigns today, he "believed in direct solicitation, asking for a specified amount, asking for gifts based on the giver's means, asking for the largest gifts first and inviting all potential donors to be part of the project"

The Origin of Philanthropy

The term *philanthropy* is derived from *philanthrōpía*, a word from Greek mythology that means "for love of humankind" (Random House 2005). Zeus, the mythological king of the gods, wished to destroy the primitive humans who lived on earth out of disdain for their weakness. However, another god, Prometheus, took pity on the creatures and gave them two transformational gifts to empower them to pursue their potential: fire, which symbolized knowledge and culture, and optimism. Using these gifts together, the humans were able to forge a better life for themselves.

The Greeks believed that all people had an obligation to advance the well-being of humankind. To fulfill one's potential, a person had to look beyond oneself and positively affect the lives of others. Prevailing modern definitions of philanthropy speak to "voluntary action for the public good" (Rooney and Nathan 2011, 118) to enable "improvement in the quality of human life" (Bremner 1988, 3). All definitions share an outward focus on voluntarily sharing personal resources to enhance the lives and well-being of others.

(Tempel 2003, 7). Through the power of community giving, the first patients were admitted to Pennsylvania Hospital, the first general hospital in the United States, in 1756 (Penn Medicine 2012).

In 1835, French historian Alexis de Tocqueville chronicled the American people's "peculiar" behavior of coming together to support the public good in his book *Democracy in America*. He noted that self-reliance was a unique and distinguishing cornerstone of American democracy and observed that "Americans of all ages, all conditions, and all dispositions constantly form associations . . . in this manner they found hospitals, prisons, and schools" (de Tocqueville 1835).

Another hundred years later, a critical shortage of hospital beds in the United States renewed the need for philanthropy. In 1946, the United States Congress passed the Hill-Burton Act to provide matching grants to remedy a critical shortage of hospital beds. However, there was a catch. To receive the grant monies, communities had to match federal dollars with dollars raised on their own. This requirement spurred community funding drives across the country. Many drives raised money in honor of soldiers and sailors who had served our nation in the recent wars, and "Memorial" was added to the names of a great number of hospitals in their memory.

In 1956, the Internal Revenue Service (IRS) determined not-for-profit healthcare organizations qualified for tax-exempt status as charitable organizations. To maintain this tax-exempt status, hospitals were required to provide medical care to those unable to pay for services; this obligation was later redefined as a responsibility to provide a broader community benefit (Nowicki 2001). While maintaining tax-exempt status has been an ongoing challenge for hospitals, it enables them to solicit funds and makes donors' contributions deductible to the fullest extent allowed by law. While tax benefits often are not among donors' primary considerations, this federal "endorsement" of charitable endeavors does appear to be correlated with securing consistent, generous support.

Building the Healthcare Fund Development Organization

Several structural models are used to facilitate philanthropy in healthcare organizations. The two prevalent models are the

- integrated hospital development department, and
- independent 501(c)(3) charitable foundation.

The foundation model has two subsets: the *separate* foundation, which is often an independent 501(c)(3) *public charity,* or the *related* foundation, which is generally a 501(c)(3) *supporting organization* controlled by the parent healthcare system. Most US healthcare foundations are *separate* foundations.

Prevalent characteristics of the foundation model include:

- The foundation's legal articles of incorporation and mission statement specify that the foundation's purpose is to support the healthcare organization by raising charitable funding.
- The community board of directors is self-perpetuating and has little or no formal affiliation with the healthcare organization.
- The foundation board maintains independence, or relative independence, in grant-making decisions.
- Foundation executives have formal or informal reporting relationships to both the foundation board and the CEO of the healthcare organization.
- Foundation executives participate in the healthcare organization's senior executive team to facilitate collaboration and stay attuned to the operational and financial issues of the supported healthcare organization.

→

- The foundation and the healthcare organization share the operational expenses (direct and indirect costs) of the fund development program. For example, foundation staff are often employed by the health system and loaned to the foundation.

Whatever model is used, the organization exists to raise, hold, and manage charitable support for the benefit of the supported healthcare organization and serves as the point of contact for individual, foundation, and corporate donors.

In the early 1960s, some community hospitals "began to hire full-time fundraising staff and create separate fundraising arms, often called foundations, to conduct fundraising on a continuous basis" (Hall 2005). However, in 1965, American healthcare materially changed after President Lyndon Johnson's campaign for compulsory health insurance led to the introduction of Medicare and Medicaid. This legislation repositioned the provision of healthcare as a basic right to be addressed by government rather than as a social responsibility to be carried out by the nonprofit sector. This philosophical shift and new reliance on third-party payers eclipsed the need and the case for community giving. Healthcare also began to be seen as a business around this time.

However, the need for philanthropy was renewed once again in 1983 when Medicare switched to prospective payment by diagnosis-related groups (DRGs), a fixed-payment schedule based on patient diagnosis that made hospitals assume more risk: If the actual cost to the hospital was more than DRG compensation, the hospital had to absorb the loss. Almost simultaneously, insurance companies began negotiating reimbursement rates with hospitals. Clearly, Medicaid and Medicare were not going to provide a sufficient stream of revenue to meet the capital needs of the nation's hospitals, and without tight cost control, healthcare organizations struggled to make money. In this era, the concept of community charitable giving regained momentum as a strategy to reduce revenue pressures and as a meaningful, reliable source of revenue. At the same time, many more hospitals started formal fund development programs to ensure a dependable revenue stream.

Characteristics of Foundations

The "independent" foundation:

- The foundation's bylaws do not restrict the foundation from giving to organizations other than the healthcare organization.
- The community board is not formally affiliated with the healthcare organization.
- The board is self-perpetuating.
- The board maintains independence in grant making.
- As a private charity, some preferential tax rules may apply to the foundation.
- Foundation assets are considered in the healthcare organization's liquidity position when the foundation is part of the obligated group.

The "closely related" foundation:

- The foundation's bylaws state that the foundation's only purpose is to support the healthcare organization.
- The foundation and the healthcare organization often have the same parent corporation.
- The foundation's board/management and the healthcare organization's board/management overlap.
- Unrestricted assets are considered in the healthcare system's liquidity position in decisions regarding credit worthiness and access to debt funding.

Since then, healthcare continues to face financial challenges spurred by legislation or economic conditions. For example, the Balanced Budget Act of 1997 reduced Medicare reimbursements, and the economic recession that began in 2008 diminished income from nonoperating investment revenues. As a result, healthcare organizations have reached a point where "wait and see" is not an option. Now is the time to position and support philanthropy in a strategic manner to achieve maximum impact.

A MEANINGFUL OPPORTUNITY

Charitable giving in the United States presents a meaningful opportunity. An annual survey of charitable giving shows gifts from all sources hover around $300 billion annually (Giving USA Foundation 2011; see Exhibit 1.1). Of that sum, more than $20 billion goes to healthcare causes—everything from hospital systems to national health charities to research organizations. However, of the $20 billion, the Association for Healthcare Philanthropy (2011a) reports total giving to hospitals and healthcare systems of about $8 billion (see Exhibit 1.2). US philanthropy has also weathered and rebounded from economic challenges; while the post-9/11 downturn and the 2008 recession prompted dips in charitable giving, both charitable giving overall and charitable giving to hospitals generally have increased year after year.

Member organizations of the Association for Healthcare Philanthropy report raising a median of about $4 million annually, a number that reflects both cash in hand and pledged commitments. While development performance varies among these organizations for a number of reasons, specialty hospitals, children's hospitals, and academic medical centers consistently raise more money than do public and community hospitals (Association for Healthcare Philanthropy 2011a).

Philanthropy delivers a strong return on investment. If the average US hospital achieves about a 2 percent operating margin, it

Exhibit 1.1: US Giving by Designation, in Billions (2010 figures)

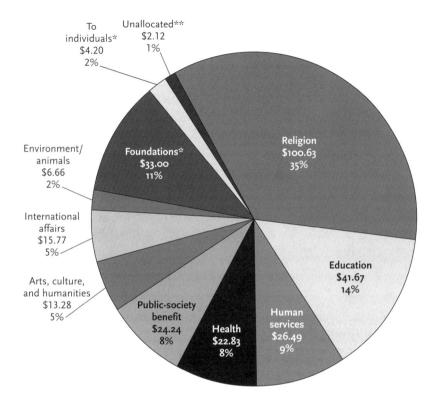

To individuals*
$4.20
2%

Unallocated**
$2.12
1%

Environment/
animals
$6.66
2%

Foundations*
$33.00
11%

Religion
$100.63
35%

International
affairs
$15.77
5%

Education
$41.67
14%

Arts, culture,
and humanities
$13.28
5%

Public-society
benefit
$24.24
8%

Health
$22.83
8%

Human
services
$26.49
9%

Source: Giving USA Foundation (2011). Used with permission.

needs to bring in $50 million in hospital gross revenue to achieve a bottom line of $1 million for reinvestment (Moody's Investors Service 2010). Philanthropy also offers a good internal rate of return. During good economic times, foundations achieving a median return on investment require only $1.36 million in gross revenue to generate $1 million in net revenue (Philanthropy Leadership Council 2005). Simply, philanthropy has the power to deliver capital at a rate of return not often possible by any clinical service line, and many healthcare systems are leveraging this strategic asset.

Exhibit 1.2: Total Funds Raised by US Hospitals and Healthcare Systems

Median Value for All Institutions

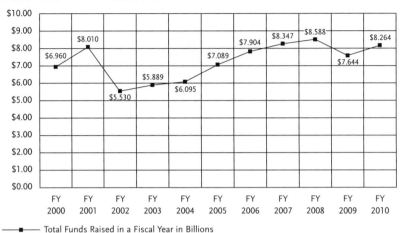

———■——— Total Funds Raised in a Fiscal Year in Billions

Source: Association for Healthcare Philanthropy (2011a). Used with permission.

Philanthropy has also been validated as a core investment strategy by ratings agencies. Moody's Investors Service (2006) issued a special comment noting its expectation that philanthropy will play a greater role in revenue generation: "We believe a strong fundraising program, as a complimentary strategy to a hospital's patient care operation, is an important consideration in our credit assessment and can positively impact bond ratings." According to the Healthcare Financial Management Association (2009), "When assessing an organization, Moody's says it considers factors such as annual unrestricted gifts, which can help support operations by supplying a steady stream of revenue. It also looks at restricted gifts earmarked for specific capital initiatives."

Healthcare philanthropy presents clear room for growth. The average hospital receives less than 1 percent of total operating revenue from philanthropic gifts, while the average university receives about 7 percent of total revenue from giving (Moody's Investors Service 2006). The fund development tools and opportunities

The Comprehensive Development Program

The comprehensive development program is an integrated continuum of strategies for engaging donors in the life of the organization. Programs include:

- **Annual giving:** These acquisition and renewal programs bring new donor support to the organization and increase loyalty among returning donors. Most gifts are unrestricted, so they may be used at the organization's discretion. Gifts are large in number but small in size and cultivated over a short period. The cost of raising money is fairly high. Annual giving programs solicit funds through mail, telephone, Internet, membership programs, tributes, events, and other methods.
- **Major gifts:** These investment-level giving programs strongly drive total dollars and return on investment. Gifts are tightly aligned to donor values and interests. Many donors restrict the use of their gifts to strategic initiatives whose fulfillment will have an evident impact. Gifts are fewer in number but larger in average size (compared to annual gifts). Cultivation time generally varies from one to fifteen years. The cost of raising a dollar hovers around 20 cents. Most gifts are secured through personal solicitation. The involvement of allies, such as executives and boards, is critical to success.
- **Planned giving:** These "ultimate" gifts often secure a donor's legacy and are an extension of the donor's values. Gifts usually are secured through direct solicitation and come in a variety of forms, such as bequests, trusts, life insurance benefits, and retirement plan assets. Cultivation of most gifts takes a long time. Planned giving brings an exceptional return on investment, but realization of such gifts is often many years away.

available to universities are equally available to healthcare organizations, so this difference in performance is largely a function of prioritization. For example, the typical university president is expected to spend a substantial amount of time cultivating philanthropy and soliciting on behalf of the institution. Universities also engaged in fundraising earlier than hospitals did.

Cash flows from a foundation are subject to year-to-year volatility, which should be considered in planning and financial forecasting. This variance is consistently attributable to outsize **major** and **planned** gifts that may not be replicable from year to year. For example, a substantial major gift received in one year may not be repeatable the next when the case for giving changes and a different set of donors is interested in that cause. By the same token, a planned gift received upon a donor's death under will is not a circumstance that can be readily predicted. However, **annual giving** funds are fairly steady and predictable. Many foundations also engage in intermittent capital campaigns that often raise many multiples of what they normally raise on an annual basis. While large capital campaigns used to be launched about once every ten years, many foundations are now in serial campaign mode.

No Tin Cup Involved

At this point, philanthropy must be distinguished from fundraising.

Fundraising generally involves a contribution given in response to a specific trigger to meet an immediate need with or without a continued relationship after the gift is made. In this way, fundraising is transactional and reactive in nature, and there is often little depth or richness to the relationship between the donor and the organization. Many hospital fund development efforts started with an acute focus on fundraising and were packed with broad-based appeals such as direct mail, special events, and other methods that present a request to be considered and then fulfilled or denied fairly immediately. While fundraising is still used to attract and acquire new donors to participate in the life of the organization, it is no longer the be-all and end-all. Rather, it has a defined place as a **first** step that enables an overall objective of building meaningful relationships expressed through philanthropy.

Philanthropy is distinguished from fundraising in that a gift is made as part of a mutually rewarding and genuine partnership that enables donors to express their core values and to meaningfully influence an outcome they care about. Philanthropy is a long-term proposition that invites donors to join the healthcare organization in a relationship that makes them part of something bigger than themselves and that promotes self-actualization and personal fulfillment. Philanthropy is a vibrant expression of passion for the organization's mission, and the way each donor supports that mission reflects his or her unique personal interests and motivations.

Leading Indicators of Success in Philanthropy

- Diversified giving strategies
- Large, loyal base of **annual** donors
- Ability to attract **major** gifts
- Multiple channels for marketing development
- Professional foundation staff
- Organizational culture of philanthropy
- Meaningful investment in development programs
- Strong involvement of board members in development
- A positive health system brand and image
- Provision of specialty services

Source: Moody's Investors Service (2006).

Philanthropy is a noble and transformative experience for donors, so organizations should never feel that they are imposing by asking someone to join their mission. They are not extending a hand in need but rather in partnership to invite someone to join them in a richly meaningful cause. Philanthropy is **not about meeting the healthcare organization's needs; it is about enabling solutions** for the greater good. There is no negative implication for the healthcare organization in advancing philanthropy; seeking philanthropic partnerships does not show a lack of strength, resolve, or solid organizational or financial management.

Shifting the focus in healthcare fund development from "fundraising" to "philanthropy" has positive implications for both donors and the organization. An approach rooted in philanthropy not only creates a more engaging and fulfilling experience for donors but also provides the healthcare organization with a more sustainable and consistent platform for performance. In this regard, all fund development efforts should ultimately be directed toward building genuine lifetime partnerships with interested community advocates rather than toward raising short-term dollars. Such relationships are facilitated by building awareness and making connections through a long-term management process known as *fund development*, which is discussed in detail later in this book.

The Fine Print

While charitable giving has great potential as a source of revenue, the caveats are worth noting:

- Securing community support through philanthropy is not as simple as turning on a faucet. While meaningful, short-term gains are possible, genuine, invested relationships that enable substantive giving usually take several years to develop.
- Philanthropy is not an even playing field. Healthcare organizations that have a national reputation, provide

Funding the Development Organization

Many considerations surround the funding of the development organization:

- The healthcare organization seeds most development efforts by funding staff and infrastructure to start a program. Once a dependable revenue stream exists, many development efforts are jointly funded by the healthcare organization and the development organization. In dividing expenses, healthcare organizations often fund overhead such as staff, office space, information technology, phones, and so forth, while development funds money-raising efforts. A caveat is most healthcare organizations invest discretionary operating dollars and may receive back gifts with a restricted purpose. Therefore, alignment of funding priorities is important to ensure charitable dollars raised are usable for the healthcare organization's priorities.
- Initiation of a development effort does not mean immediate availability of contributed funds. While incremental short-term gains are achievable, donor relationships take time to build. The largest gifts are cultivated as a result of building trust and demonstrating stewardship over time.
- Fund development usually does not reach a point of diminishing return. The more you invest, the more you receive back. Inadequate funding of the development organization often delays results that could have been achieved sooner. Investment and planning must be coordinated to enable smart and methodical growth.
- If the healthcare organization has to make budget cuts, it should keep a long-term view in mind when considering reducing funding to development—especially regarding staff cuts. It takes time to build trusting relationships. When development staff are cut, key relationships are set back. Cuts to save money today can negatively affect charitable revenue for a long time.

specialty clinical services such as oncology and pediatrics, offer academic medicine programs, and have sophisticated development offices are generally most effective at securing contributions. Consequently, organizations facing the most acute financial pressures (and thus needing the most revenue from charitable giving) often have less potential to attract charitable dollars because donors tend to invest in enabling excellence rather than in abating need. However, the relative opportunity for each healthcare organization makes philanthropy an essential endeavor.

- Donors' confidence has diminished in recent years as a result of the poor economy and scandals involving the misuse or mismanagement of charitable funds. Transparency and disclosure to donors and engagement of senior executives in philanthropy are more important than ever to restoring or maintaining donors' trust that their contributions will be managed and used well.

The Giving Vortex

A *vortex* is a spiral column, such as a whirlpool, that pulls matter tightly into its eye through an irresistible force. In the **giving vortex** (Exhibit 1.3), the power of relationships pulls donors more and more tightly into the institution's embrace and toward greater levels of giving. However, for donors to make increasingly significant gifts to the organization, they must have the **financial ability** to do so and the healthcare organization's projects must be endeavors that align with the donors' personal **value affinities** and interests. All growth is ultimately grounded in **steward-ship,** which demonstrates integrity, sound financial management, and an ability to achieve results.

Exhibit 1.3: The Giving Vortex

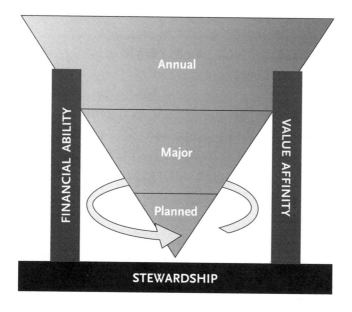

IN SUMMARY

An onslaught of financial challenges driven by legislation, relationships with insurance providers, and general economic conditions are pressuring healthcare organizations to find additional sources of dependable revenue to shore up existing operations and enable future growth and profitability. Philanthropy is a viable revenue stream with a solid return on investment that can enable organizational strength and sustainability. To leverage this opportunity, healthcare organizations must focus on efforts that advance long-term strategies rooted in philanthropy rather than become mired in short-term fundraising. Instead of relying on a stable of special events or mass-marketing campaigns, organizations need to direct their fund development efforts toward building relationships with potential donors. Healthcare organizations also have an opportunity to follow the university dictum of making philanthropy a high strategic priority that merits president/CEO involvement.

STEPS TO CREATING A PLATFORM
FOR PERFORMANCE

The following chapters of this book explore levers that support and advance healthcare philanthropy. The end of each chapter features a list of actions that will help CEOs, board members, and other key allies attract a more vibrant stream of charitable revenue and thereby advance their noble missions to heal.

Interview with Richard L. Clarke, DHA, FHFMA,
Healthcare Financial Management Association President
and CEO

QUESTION: What value do you feel philanthropy could offer in strengthening and sustaining the financial condition of our healthcare organizations?

ANSWER: Philanthropy has always been an important part of the operations of not-for-profit healthcare organizations, providing necessary funding for new services, capital improvements, and shoring up decreasing financial positions.

Many organizations look at their capital planning as a three-legged stool: One leg is funding from operations, the other is the issuance of debt, and the third is philanthropy. A balanced organization will look at all of these approaches and determine what makes the most sense from a strategic and operational perspective.

→

QUESTION: What advice do you have for healthcare CEOs who are considering what the role of philanthropy should be in their organization?

ANSWER: As with any initiative, you must set the tone from the top. For philanthropy to be successful, it needs to be led by the members of the community and supported by the executive team. The C-suite is an integral part of this, from the CEO to the CFO and all other members of the team.

Appropriate resourcing for the development department is critical based upon the strategic fundraising plan and the type of funds you are raising to support the needs of your community. There is a vast difference in the resources needed to support a small auxiliary versus a major multi-million-dollar capital campaign. Depending on the type of funds and the sophistication of the donors, you will need to consider event planning, communication, and development expertise to bring into the organization.

Philanthropy has been, and always will be, an important part of not only the financial and strategic plans of healthcare organizations, but an excellent tool for community engagement and building patient loyalty.

The more the community feels a part of the organization, the more they become a stakeholder and consider it "my health provider," which builds patient affinity and a positive sense of ownership within the community.

PART II

Key Partners in the Philanthropy Endeavor

CHAPTER 2

Leveraging the Healthcare CEO in Philanthropy

For many development executives,
getting the CEO to "get it" is the key hurdle
to improving development performance.

—*Philanthropy Leadership Council*

MEANINGFUL ENGAGEMENT IN philanthropy is essential to raising capital, fostering community ownership, and maximizing an organization's potential. An evaluation of the development role of the university president says it best: "No other institutional officer can create the vision, establish [organization]-wide priorities, or make the case as effectively as the president. . . . Because of the key visioning and priority-setting roles the president plays, the ultimate responsibility for any fundraising cannot be delegated to the staff, the [governing] board or the foundation board" (Hodson 2010).

Philanthropy has become a lever to organizational excellence and can no longer be an optional role for the CEO. The CEO is entrusted with the successful management and financial health of the organization, so it naturally follows that he or she is obligated to take on a meaningful role in fund development.

The importance of the healthcare CEO in positioning philanthropy for internal and external success cannot be overstated. The CEO is the embodiment of the organization's mission and is the face of the organization in the community. He or she is uniquely positioned to make donors confident of the organization's strength, vision, plans, and ability to execute. On a human level, the CEO is best positioned to make donors feel personally valued, connected, and respected and to convey the importance of their role in advancing the organization. The CEO's support is also essential to driving internal organizational support for philanthropy.

CHALLENGES TO PARTICIPATION

Despite their considerable influence and gravitas, many CEOs express a lack of willingness or ability to help with philanthropy. Common objections include:

- "The board has other priorities for my time."
- "My plate is already more than full."
- "I hired a foundation person to handle that function."
- "I would be embarrassed to ask someone for money."
- "I don't socialize with people who would give."
- "I'm not sure how to help."

Of these objections, two are most problematic: lack of available time and lack of comfort in the philanthropy role (Philanthropy Leadership Council 2005).

The Challenge of Time

The countless demands placed on today's healthcare CEOs understandably create time constraints. Some CEOs say they simply cannot find the time to add development to a packed schedule.

Time is an issue in some part because the majority of boards of directors do not prioritize philanthropy relative to work in other areas, such as clinical quality, safety, service, or operational effectiveness. A 2010 Association for Healthcare Philanthropy survey found only 36 percent of hospitals include philanthropy among the list of responsibilities in the CEO's official job description (Page 2011). If participation in philanthropy is becoming a key leadership activity, it should be a function the board honors and evaluates as part of the CEO role. By adding philanthropy to the CEO's formal list of expectations, the board quantifies the value of allocating time to the activity.

The CEO who limits involvement in philanthropy because he or she does not see its financial potential or value relative to other activities may be creating a self-fulfilling prophecy. The typical hospital CEO devotes less than 5 percent of his or her time to

---

Lessons from a University President

University development programs may be a model worth considering. Collegiate fundraising in the United States started with Harvard College president Henry Dunster in 1640 and has since become increasingly formalized and systematic (Cook and Lasher 1996). The first institutionally related foundation in a university setting was established at Kansas University in 1891. Private universities started hiring development officers in the 1920s (Cook and Lasher 1996), and today they prioritize philanthropy on the university president's agenda. While universities benefit from having a built-in group of prospects—alumni spread over a geographical area that is usually larger than the typical healthcare organization's service area—universities and healthcare organizations have access to the same development programs and relationship-building tools.

---

philanthropy, and the typical hospital receives less than 1 percent of its total operating revenue from philanthropic gifts. In contrast, the typical university president spends more than 30 percent of his or her time on philanthropy, and the average university receives 7 percent of its total revenue from gifts. While the ability to effectively raise money is considered a prerequisite for today's college or university president, that mentality has not yet taken root in healthcare.

The benefits of a top-level focus on fund development are clear. While few, if any, healthcare CEOs work a 40-hour workweek, consider philanthropy's financial potential if the healthcare CEO devoted just 10 percent of a standard workweek—four hours—to interactions with donors and key constituencies. While that level of commitment might be unrealistic at first, holding any consistent block of time inviolate would be a significant step toward advancing philanthropy.

The Challenge of Comfort

Other CEOs do not allocate time for philanthropy because they find the role uncomfortable. Most healthcare CEOs are high-performing individuals who are not accustomed to failure, so lack of comfort can be a significant barrier to participation. Some CEOs avoid participation in development simply because they do not feel they have the tools and training, while others feel they do not have the interpersonal skills.

A CEO who has a heart for the work can quickly be brought up to speed. It is helpful for CEOs to understand the dynamics of the major gifts process and how a solicitation visit may flow. He or she should be informed of typical concerns and objections a donor may share—a subject covered in this book's chapter on solicitation—and be prepared to respond to these questions. Role play in mock solicitations—particularly solicitations asking for a specific sum—may help CEOs express themselves and "experience" a donor visit. It is also helpful for CEOs to understand the behind-the-scenes, internal roles in which they can make an appreciable difference—from building culture to enabling access to strategic information. While internal roles are often more "guts than glory," they set the stage for the success of overall efforts.

A CEO who is uncomfortable building relationships presents a different set of challenges. Most CEOs have the interpersonal skills needed: good manners, active listening, respect for others, and the ability to express the organization's vision. To gain confidence in the role, the CEO may wish to find roles within the spectrum of development activities that play to his or her strengths. For example, the CEO may focus his or her primary involvement on public speaking or on building relationships. In rare cases, the CEO does not have the social skills or attitude to successfully participate in cultivation and solicitation, and high-level surrogates who can assist in these capacities (e.g., other senior executives, board leaders, physicians) need to be engaged—though no surrogate can replace the power and the prestige of the CEO.

The most successful philanthropy organizations are not focused on raising money but on creating strong, meaningful relationships with donors who want to positively influence health outcomes in their communities. When philanthropy is put in that context, many CEOs find the prospect of fund development activities less daunting.

If the CEO dedicates time and gains confidence in his or her skills, professional development staff—including the chief development officer (CDO) and major gifts and planned-giving officers—can leverage that time and involvement. Development staff facilitates high-value interactions by identifying the best prospects and engaging the CEO at key, meaningful points in the relationship. The development team can also provide necessary briefings and background information to enable the CEO to join the conversation as an informed and confident player.

HIGH-IMPACT PHILANTHROPY ACTIVITIES
FOR THE CEO

Optimized CEO involvement is much more than appearances at foundation functions or delivery of a few words about giving at a local civic group meeting. It is about

- making a case: creating and sharing a strategically aligned, compelling case for support;
- cultivating relationships: instilling trust and confidence in the institution through genuine interaction with donors and community allies; and
- promoting an organizational culture that supports and extends philanthropy.

Separate chapters of this book are devoted to these focus areas. In this chapter, we explore them from the perspective of CEO involvement.

Fostering Relationships

In the relationship-building capacity, the CEO brings stature and prestige to education, cultivation, and solicitation activities. Broad-based activities include making remarks at foundation functions and educating the public about the essential role of philanthropy in strengthening and sustaining the healthcare organization. Most valuable, however, is the CEO's role in building relationships with donors who have the affinity and ability to make a major gift.

Veteran fund development leader Frank Hall (2005) said, "Successful major gift fundraising doesn't occur until a potential donor has developed a relationship with the institutional leadership. Major donors have every right to expect to develop a relationship with the hospital CEO." Those making or considering substantial investments in an organization's vision naturally want to meet the individual who will advance and implement that vision. CEO involvement also demonstrates respect to those who are or would be the organization's staunchest allies. A key potential donor passed off to a subordinate surrogate may feel disrespected or even slighted.

In advancing relationships with major gift donors, the CEO shares the organization's strategic vision and explains the impact of charitable dollars on the health system. The CEO also participates as part of a solicitation team on calls to prospective donors. Even in this capacity, the CEO's usual role is to convey the vision of the institution, not to ask for dollars. He or she explains the proposed initiative, the due diligence behind the planning process, the reason the healthcare organization feels it is best prepared to advance the project, and the anticipated community benefit of the initiative. The CEO also shares plans and timelines for implementation, discloses the organization's own financial investment in the project, and assures donors of the long-term sustainability of the project so that donors have confidence in the plans for implementation. CEOs should be prepared to explain the fundamentals of healthcare finance to donors if asked. Many investment-level donors want to understand the basic financial structure and revenue streams of the organization and its rationale for philanthropy.

In a stewardship role, the CEO thanks donors who have made a gift to the organization with a handwritten note, a phone call, or a more structured interaction. He or she assures donors that the organization will use or has used their money in a way consistent with their wishes and that the initiative is moving forward as proposed. Ongoing stewardship is also an opportunity for the CEO to affirm how important community donors are to the mission. Ultimately, the CEO's engagement in philanthropy conveys unequaled gravitas and credibility in forming, nurturing, and sustaining organizational relationships.

Model Giving

An essential piece of successful personal solicitation is the CEO's own personal gift. Careful consideration must be given to the amount the CEO invests. CEOs set a pace in the organization, so they need to give at a level commensurate with the contribution other employees are being asked to make. For example, many campaigns ask employees to consider a leadership gift that represents a level playing field—such as one hour's pay per pay period, which is roughly equivalent to 1 percent of base pay. If that standard is established, CEOs need to contribute that amount before the campaign starts to show their commitment. Some CEOs calculate the math and balk at the result, but they must keep in mind that the gift should be larger—even disproportionate—to other gifts they make.

The CEO's personal gift needs to reflect his or her stature in the community and be commensurate with what community donors consider appropriate. The community knows the CEO earns a high salary, and thus it perceives he or she has the financial capacity to make a meaningful gift. For organizations whose public nature means the details of compensation are shared in the local media, the community may also see that the CEO receives bonuses and other incentives. The community will not look favorably on a CEO whose gift is not commensurate with what those of similar circumstances but with no official ties to the organization are being asked to consider.

CEOs may also wish to consider the use of any gift they make. While at times a CEO's visible support is needed for a particular community campaign, giving to one service line as opposed to another may also be an internal political liability for a CEO. He or she may want to give consistently to the "unrestricted" or "greatest need" fund and leave the use of the gift to the discretion of the foundation board. The CEO could also designate that his or her gift be used to offset the foundation's operating expenses; in so doing, the gift effectively multiplies by enabling fund development efforts. Or, the CEO's gift could support aspects of the mission to which he or she feels a personal connection; CEOs should have the same opportunity that other donors have to give to causes consistent with their values and interests.

While personal giving is a sensitive subject, it is an area in which it would benefit CEOs to think about why they do what they do and to be able to articulate those thoughts if asked, which donors often do.

Leverage Allies

The success of the major gifts program strongly correlates not only with the involvement of the CEO but also with the involvement of community board members, physicians, and other senior executives.

The CEO plays a primary role in engaging and empowering allies, and a great deal of this role is communicating that philanthropy is an essential part of the organization rather than just "nice to have" and setting and modeling expectations for personal engagement.

Engaging Board Members

Enfranchising governing and foundation boards of directors in the fund development process helps engage some of the greatest potential allies. The CEO generally has the most substantive relationship with the healthcare organization's governing board, so he or she is the best person to explain the rationale for philanthropy and to ask for the board's engagement in philanthropy as an aspect of sound governance. The CEO can also

- explain that fund development is part of the role during board recruitment,
- include philanthropy in new board member orientation,
- seek to have philanthropy included in the board member job description,
- ensure philanthropy is routinely included in board meeting agendas and reports,
- put metrics for fund development on dashboards that the board reviews,

- provide educational opportunities on philanthropy and solicitation,
- invite donors to board meetings and other forums and give them an opportunity to explain why they gave, and
- have a representative from the governing board sit on the foundation board and vice versa to act as a liaison and facilitate alignment and collaboration.

Furthermore, the CEO has an opportunity to coach the governing board that the presence of a foundation board or development council to champion fund development does not mean governing board members can forego their own responsibility to foster giving through direct engagement in fund development activities. The foundation board or development council can also extend its reach by having additional community leadership volunteers work on philanthropy.

While the importance of the foundation board's/development council's role in guiding and facilitating fund development should have been communicated to members when they were recruited, the CEO should reaffirm the role as vital to the future of the healthcare organization. Board members leading fund development should be empowered as stewards of philanthropic dollars. By creating an environment of mutual respect and collaboration, the CEO can inspire and motivate foundation and development board members to be advocates for the organization.

Finally, many volunteer board members say their participation in fund development is in part contingent on seeing organizational leaders model and advance philanthropy. Leadership participation generally unfolds from the inside out, again placing the CEO in the position of role model and expectation setter.

Engaging Physicians

The CEO can also encourage physicians to become champions for philanthropy. Physicians are largely independent contractors who can choose to participate in the life of the healthcare organization or not. Because physicians are well-positioned to share the clinical case for giving and often have the greatest influence on grateful patients, their engagement in philanthropy is crucial.

In seeking the involvement of physicians, CEOs have a handful of opportunities that offer the most traction:

- They can communicate the role of philanthropy to physicians individually and collectively so that they truly understand the impact of community giving on acquiring capital and fueling advancement.
- They can ask physicians to consider becoming donors, ambassadors, and petitioners to create a stronger healthcare organization and a better place for them to serve their patients.
- Physicians can be recruited for specific endeavors. For example, a CEO can personally ask an inspiring, respected physician leader to be a champion for a funding priority in the physician's area of practice.
- CEOs can honor physicians who participate in public and hospital forums. For example, they can be recognized in medical staff or section meetings that include their professional peers and in the boardroom that represents the wider community, and their names can be placed on physician honor rolls or displays in areas physicians frequent, such as the doctors' lounge or the path from the physician parking area into the building.

Engaging Executives

The CEO has the ability to direct the activities of the healthcare organization's executive staff by setting their goals, influencing their priorities, and evaluating their performance. The CEO has the power to set an expectation of executive leadership participation and buy-in by including philanthropy in executives' performance goals and as a metric. By communicating that philanthropy is part of everyone's job and by directing the executive team to cascade that understanding throughout the organization, the CEO has the ability to influence fund development on a broad scale.

Elucidate the Financial Case

The financial underpinnings of the modern healthcare organization are complex and difficult to explain. Often community members (and even board members) do not entirely understand how a not-for-profit healthcare organization receives money, the sources from which the system receives money, and the role that voluntary charitable contributions play. While the intricacies of commercial insurers and government payers are too complicated to explain in full, the CEO can educate the community on the healthcare organization's status as a nonprofit that relies on philanthropic support to progress. Part of this message may address prevalent misconceptions that the organization is substantially supported by tax dollars from the city, county, state, or federal government. It is also valuable to describe the organization's responsibility to provide charity care to those who do not have adequate coverage and to offer other community benefits. Finally, the CEO may want to explain that the operating margin the organization achieves as excess revenues over expenses is fully reinvested in the organization.

INTERNAL ROLES

High-value internal roles for the CEO include defining and nurturing a culture conducive to philanthropy, positioning the development function for credibility and access, aligning development strategically to optimize project selection and impact, and championing an adequate (and sometimes disproportionate) operational budget. These roll-up-your-sleeves roles behind the scenes can do as much to create a platform for performance as the roles in the limelight. Most are more about buy-in and leadership than face time.

Nurture Culture

John Miller, FACHE, has been the chief executive officer of AnMed Health in Anderson, South Carolina, for 14 years. His hospital identification badge says a lot about him and his leadership commitments in a single glance. Instead of indicating his title as president or CEO, his badge shows his role: "nurturing culture." And nurture culture he does.

Visionary CEOs like John Miller know that engaged participation in and advocacy for philanthropy by a CEO signal to others

---

High-Value Activities for the Healthcare CEO

- Nurture a culture of philanthropy that advances giving as a vital endeavor.
- Engage employees, physicians, and boards through expectations and modeling.
- Affirm the importance of donors' and development volunteers' roles to the organization's mission.
- Enable strategic alignment to optimize project selection and impact.
- Include philanthropy in strategic and operational plans.
- Ensure adequate—and sometimes disproportionate—investment in development.
- Position the development function and the CDO for credibility and access.
- Meet with the CDO consistently to discuss strategy and plans for advancing philanthropy.
- Include performance indicators for philanthropy on organizational dashboards.
- Share the case for support in the hospital and in the community.
- Emphasize the importance of giving in meetings and communications.

---

that the development function is a vital endeavor. Once again, the CEO, symbolic of leadership, can create positive repercussions throughout the organization by

- routinely sharing the impact of and need for philanthropy,
- ensuring all employees at all levels are asked to consider a gift,
- engaging employees through role modeling and advocacy,
- setting an expectation that everyone has a role in philanthropy,
- including philanthropy in senior leaders' and organizational goals,
- showing philanthropy has priority status on the institutional agenda,
- ensuring philanthropy is part of strategic and financial plans,
- including development metrics on hospital performance dashboards, and
- celebrating those in the hospital who have helped secure gifts.

Another lever a CEO has in building culture is even stronger than those in the previous list: positioning the development function and the CDO for internal credibility and access to emerging strategic plans, board members, and so forth. High-value activities to this end include

- placing the CDO on the executive team to facilitate information sharing and relationships and to show importance of the function;
- giving the development leader a senior title that conveys credibility;
- maintaining regular communication and face-to-face interaction with the CDO to build a collaborative relationship and to discuss strategy, plans, priorities, and expectations;
- ensuring the CDO has access to emerging and current strategy and plans;
- including information about giving in board and management meetings; and

- introducing the CDO to organizational allies/contacts with potential to give.

With the right cultural environment and a high-functioning working relationship built on mutual respect in place, the CEO and CDO can work closely as partners in advancing community relationships to fund the vision.

Enable Alignment

Alignment of philanthropic priorities and the healthcare organization's strategic vision is critical to optimizing the impact of charitable giving. The CEO has an opportunity to foster alignment by

- ensuring development is "at the table" for key meetings about strategy,
- sharing the strategic plan with both foundation board and CDO,
- insisting grant requests to the foundation flow from the strategic plan, and
- adhering to a clear and systematic process to identify funding priorities.

Tight alignment ensures contributions are used for initiatives that will best advance the overall organization rather than for projects that drift from the mission, are tangential, or have minimal value. Alignment also means the CEO has best exercised his or her fiduciary duty.

Champion Investment

When return on investment from philanthropy is benchmarked against return on investment from clinical service lines, many hospitals find that their philanthropy return is a more effectively generated dollar. Even so, as priorities compete for a place in healthcare system budgets, clinical revenue centers tend to win out over seemingly administrative cost centers such as fund development. The fund development function, however, is also a revenue center in which an investment benefits the greater organization.

The CEO can ensure the development function is positioned as a revenue center that merits investment. He or she can also ensure the development function receives adequate—and sometimes disproportionate—budget and staff resources to build or expand its programs.

An article on the challenges of investing in fund development states well the case for ensuring investment early on:

> [T]he only element holding up success in securing charitable support is funding the cost of fundraising. Unfortunately, success in fundraising does not come immediately with the investment of added operational resources. . . . It is not like turning on the faucet and having gift funding flow to the institution. Relationships with prospective donors must come first and most often take time.
>
> As seasoned professionals responsible for building philanthropy programs know so well, the return on the investment can take months or years. However, if the investment is delayed or does not use every resource available, the return will be less than the potential and slower to materialize than expected or required. To make money requires an investment . . . (Holmes and Hodson 2010)

The CEO's advocacy is also important when operational budget cuts must be made—a frequent occurrence in the economic downturn that began in 2008. Decisions about cutting development should be made with a long-term view in mind—especially with regard to potential staff cuts. A cut to save money today can have negative financial implications for a long time. It takes time to onboard development staff and build genuine, trusting relationships. When development staff are cut, key relationships are set back, and the organization loses time later hiring and onboarding new talent. When possible, a staffing level should be maintained to support the program's long-term needs and aspirations.

While investments in philanthropy are well placed in securing a return, most healthcare organizations invest unrestricted operating dollars to fund the foundation and receive back a large percentage of charitable gifts restricted for a specific purpose. Some organizations may want to consider this factor when deciding how much they can invest and still meet other organizational needs.

An issue related to investment is selection of a business model for the foundation—"who" invests "what" to build and sustain the development enterprise. Often healthcare organizations and foundations share the expenses. The hospital usually funds overhead costs, such as salaries, benefits, office space, telephones, computer services, and accounting services, while the foundation funds the costs of implementing and executing development programs. While this division of expenses is the convention, funding norms should be determined on the basis of

- control (some hospitals choose to fund all expenses of the charitable arm primarily to make it dependent or to exercise greater influence), and
- alignment (some fund the foundation endeavor to ensure that foundation grants and hospital needs are aligned—almost a quid pro quo that support is contingent on the foundation making an impact).

The objective in providing funding should be to build capacity and expand the philanthropy program to enable it to meet the healthcare organization's overall development needs and reach its development potential.

IN SUMMARY

The CEO's engagement in practical and symbolic development roles is critical for an effort to flourish. The CEO is a major player in engaging donors, facilitating allies, and creating an internal environment that supports and enables giving. While others can fill these roles, the influence of the CEO is unmatchable.

Five Steps to Creating a Platform for Performance

1. **Make it official.** Ask the governing board of the organization to consider including explicit philanthropy roles in the CEO's job description so that time and priority are given to development activities and everyone has a mutual understanding of the CEO's responsibilities in advancing philanthropy.
2. **Dedicate time.** Set aside an inviolable block of time on your weekly calendar to meet with donors. For example, block an hour every Tuesday morning or 90 minutes every Friday at lunch. Prioritize these meetings when conflicts arise or when you are seeking time on the calendar for other appointments. Never reschedule a meeting with a donor once it is set unless a mission-critical task arises.
3. **Get comfortable.** Build your skills and understanding of the fund development and solicitation process so you can comfortably and confidently participate. Then get out there and try your wings. Once you have been on a few calls, you'll probably find that your time with donors is affirming and fun. If you need additional help, your foundation staff should be able to provide training and other resources. Professional organizations, including the American College of Healthcare Executives and the Association for Healthcare Philanthropy, offer classes and information on philanthropy specifically designed for CEOs.
4. **Use your assets.** Foster a partnership with the CDO through routine communication and interaction. Bring the CDO to community functions and charity events so he or she can introduce you to key donors and inform your interactions. Include the CDO on the executive leadership team to bring

the community and donor perspective to the decision-making table.

5. **Give at a level that makes you proud.** Make your healthcare organization one of your top three philanthropic priorities. Your annual gift advances an organization in which you have a vested interest and supports a cause aligned with your personal values and interests. When you give generously, you inspire staff and the community to do the same.

CHAPTER 3

Positioning Board Members to Fulfill Their Purpose as Powerful Advocates

[Board members] are the primary stewards of the spirit
of philanthropy. As stewards, they are the legendary
"keepers of the hall." They hold the nonprofit organization
in trust to ensure that it will continue to function
according to the dictates of the mission.

—*Henry A. Rosso, founder of The Fund Raising School*

A CADRE OF committed, informed board members and leadership volunteers can be a healthcare foundation's greatest asset. While
these allies juggle a realm of other responsibilities to devote time to
philanthropy, their positions as connected and respected community leaders and objective volunteers give them significant credibility
in approaching prospective donors.

Board members—whether of the healthcare organization or
the foundation organization—provide governance that protects,
guides, and advances the mission. Part of that responsibility is
ensuring sound fiduciary leadership for the organization, including
making decisions on the use and appropriate management of organizational funds. There is a clear corollary here: To *invest* adequate
funds to ensure fulfillment of the mission, board members must
accept responsibility to *secure* adequate funds. Board members have

a clear leadership role in fostering philanthropy to enable the continued viability of the nonprofit healthcare organization.

UNIQUELY POSITIONED FOR TRANSFORMATIONAL LEADERSHIP

Board members have unique capabilities to galvanize the greater community to support the mission. They breathe life into the mission by explaining the work to members of the community and asking them to become involved. To ideally serve as leaders and advocates, board members must embrace three roles in advancing philanthropy:

- *Engaging:* ensuring thoughtful involvement and attendance
- *Giving:* making an annual financial gift commensurate with ability
- *Connecting:* fostering connections with potential donors by advocating for the mission and leveraging personal networks

The Role of Engaging

Thoughtful involvement and attendance are board members' most basic responsibilities. Board members bring their time, attention, and intelligence to the task of guiding the organization and acting as stewards. To do this work well, board members must, at a minimum

- learn the organization's mission, vision, values, programs, and plans;
- attend and actively participate in board and committee meetings;
- guide the creation of sound policies, procedures, and plans;
- share their ideas for innovation and advancement;

- raise any concerns and ask for clarification;
- ensure the organization operates in an ethical manner;
- steward the financial resources of the organization;
- represent the organization at events and other gatherings; and
- hire and support the foundation executive.

The Role of Giving

Board leaders have an up-close view of the intricacies of the health-care organization. Accordingly, they are creators or endorsers of organizational plans and priorities. Board leaders are also acutely aware of the organization's financial resources and the gap that often exists between what is available and what is needed to fuel excellence. Because they have this ownership and insight, the community expects the board of directors to step up first in charitable giving to advance the mission. Every board member who makes an annual financial contribution commensurate with his or her ability demonstrates confidence in the mission and serves as an essential example and inspiration to others in the community who may be asked to join in the work.

Having this incredible opportunity to motivate their peers and others, board members who are unwilling to make a financial gift for any reason (e.g., the organization is not one of their philanthropic priorities, or they feel their volunteer time is an adequate replacement for a financial gift) are problematic. Many donors expect those closest to the organization to have the greatest confidence in its future and thus a lack of board investment sends a strong negative signal to the community and potential funders and makes board members with such an outlook more of a liability than an asset. Boards of directors must adhere to high standards of membership and address this issue head-on. Those who do not want to participate should be asked to gracefully resign.

A prolific author on fund development issues aptly conveyed the symbolic value and importance of leaders' support: "[T]he manner in which we use money expresses something about who we are and what we value, about how our own personal philanthropy—the dollar amount we contribute to the institution whose care has been entrusted to us—reflects our valuation of the institution" (Henderson 2003).

The Role of Connecting

Board members and their allies have an opportunity to transform the healthcare organization by inviting the community to become partners in philanthropy. This role—to identify, educate, cultivate, solicit, and steward top prospects and donors—is the board's most noble purpose. This overall objective comprises a variety of functions, including

- infusing credibility,
- creating connections,
- raising sights, and
- solidifying partnerships.

Let's look at each of these functions in more detail.

Infusing Credibility

Board members have unparalleled credibility when making the case for support and asking for a gift. They have the advantage of being seen as objective parties because they derive no direct personal or professional benefit from the cause; they are impartial advocates who participate purely out of belief in the value of the organization's mission. While senior hospital executives have gravitas in conversations with potential donors, they may be perceived as having a vested interest in the outcome.

Board members typically are the social, business, or civic peers of the individuals and corporate leaders the foundation wishes to engage. As peers, they tend to participate in the same civic and social activities and organizations. More important, they often have similar financial status to that of the people they wish to approach. This congruity levels the playing field for leadership volunteers as they reach out to the community.

Donors are drawn to organizations that attract strong board leadership. When donors scan a roster of board members on an organization's letterhead or website, the names of people they respect or know inspire confidence. If people they respect have shared their valuable time and expertise as members of the board, they reason that the cause must be worthwhile.

Creating Connections

Board members are essential to creating a broad network of prospective donors. The engagement of board members enables the nonprofit organization to cultivate and sustain hundreds of meaningful relationships. The capacity of the organization to do so is greatly hampered if paid staff are the only connection between the organization and its constituencies. The full-on participation of board members in the identification, cultivation, solicitation, and stewardship of donors has a viral effect that increases an organization's reach. Board members are key allies because people give to people: to friends, to colleagues, to those they trust will do the right thing.

Personal connection to someone in the organization is an important consideration in deciding which prospects would be most likely to enter into a relationship. Board members often have an unmatched ability to "get their foot in the door." The hardest part of any solicitation process is gaining a face-to-face audience with the prospective donor, and a board member's access, personal relationships, and credibility can be considerable enablers. Board members who are reticent to accompany the gift officer on visits can still contribute to the effort in a meaningful way by calling a prospective donor and setting up the visit for the gift officer, effectively turning a cold call into a "warm" call. Having a board member call a personal contact and say, "I'd love for you to meet with our gift officer about an exciting project" is more effective than having an unfamiliar gift officer call the contact out of the blue. Board member involvement in this respect is better than no involvement at all.

Raising Sights

Board members are often positioned to challenge their peers through their own personal giving. As has already been noted, board members' financial means often are commensurate with those of the peers they solicit, enabling them to ask for a commitment equal to the one they have made. This influence can be powerful; people's desire to emulate the "normative" behavior of those they respect or consider peers is a strong motivator. Again, while the healthcare organization's executives may have equal financial power to that of the people they are soliciting, this challenge does not carry the same weight when proposed by senior organizational leaders because donors often see executives' gifts as a base expectation of their position.

Solidifying Partnerships

Board members often have the greatest impact through involvement in personal solicitation, especially for major gifts. While most annual giving programs, such as direct mail or online giving, can be ably executed by the foundation staff, the involvement of board leaders is essential to a successful major gifts program because no solicitation is more compelling than that of a volunteer peer. In fact, the success of major gifts programs is strongly correlated with the direct involvement of community volunteer leaders. To be successful in this frontline advocacy role, board members need to be well-informed about the healthcare organization's strategic vision and able to convey a case for support that inspires prospective community partners to help the organization achieve its goals.

Fund development is not just about solicitation. It is about a continuum of activities that enhance the healthcare organization's relationship with the community and create the capacity for organizational advancement. Identifying, connecting, educating, and thanking donors are all powerful roles, so board members who are

Making Sense of the Mission

When community volunteer leaders go out and build partnerships with others to enhance and expand a healthcare organization's mission, they will be most effective if they keep in mind what the organization's mission is really about:

- Restoring the innocence and hope of childhood
- Enabling people to fulfill their highest potential or long-held dreams
- Enhancing people's ability to move, run, feel, or think
- Keeping families together

The mission is not so much about MRIs, surgery, and prevention programs as it is about the people whose lives are touched and changed by those services. At the end of the day, the potential to improve people's lives is why healthcare organizations do what they do and why board members ask others to be part of this healing work. When one taps into the passion to save and change people's lives, one can move mountains.

apprehensive about asking for contributions should be able to find a role along that continuum in which they feel confident.

SETTING THE STANDARD AT EXCELLENCE

A transformational board thinks highly of its work. As such, it sets a standard of excellence in all its endeavors. It selects new members thoughtfully to ensure they are prepared and able to fulfill all desired aspects of board leadership. The board also insists on having the training and information it needs to enable each member to successfully advance its noble work.

Selecting Well

To fulfill these important roles, self-perpetuating boards can strategically recruit members who have the specific skills and connections necessary to advance the current and future needs of the institution. To that end, it is inherent that healthcare organizations and healthcare foundations make their expectations of board members with regard to philanthropy clear at the start. Advancing philanthropy is a core responsibility of building the capacity and ensuring the financial stability of the mission. Historically, however, board members' role in philanthropy has been downplayed to secure candidates' participation on the board. When a prospective board member cites his or her lack of comfort in the role and the response is something akin to "Don't worry about it," "It's okay if you aren't part of it," or "It's not a big part of what we do," this precedent deflates the board's motivation to engage others in the mission. While refocusing on the mission may be a difficult cultural adjustment, hospitals need to develop such moxie about the mission's importance that they insist board members be fully engaged in all aspects of leadership.

Engagement and passion for an organization are exemplified by any college football game on a Saturday afternoon. Fans not only wear their team's colors but sometimes go so far as to paint their faces in honor of the team. So a simple litmus test is: Do board members have enough passion for the mission that they would "paint their faces" for the organization? Organizations need to have enough pride in their mission to tell new hospital and foundation board members that a key part of their role is not only sustaining the mission but strengthening it to ensure its continuity and vibrancy long into the future.

The classic Disney truism for hiring selection applies here, too. Disney's philosophy is that it is simply not enough for candidates to "fog a mirror." In other words, warm breath and a warm pulse do not excellence make, and leadership volunteers should be selected with the same degree of diligence one would exercise when selecting a key employee. The Ritz-Carlton has a similar philosophy in that it "hires slowly" and "fires quickly." A board that respects itself and its membership seeks to achieve individual and collective excellence.

Board member selection also offers distinct opportunities for some public healthcare organizations that have separate foundation organizations. Some public organizations have politically appointed or prewired methods for selecting board members, which means members may be selected with an eye for meeting other objectives and fulfilling other qualifications than those generally deemed optimal for a fund development role. Having a separate and self-perpetuating foundation board sometimes enables the inclusion of other leaders who have the community stature, broad networks, and financial capacity ideal for a philanthropy advocate.

Enabling Success

Board members who offer their time and leverage their connections deserve to have ample tools and information at their disposal. To that end, the healthcare organization and fund development organization must proactively meet board member needs by doing the following:

- *Sharing detailed information about hospital strategy and plans.*
  While this type of information is sometimes "top secret," the savvy healthcare organization never moves forward with important plans without engaging the best and the brightest it has. Both foundation and healthcare boards of directors need and deserve to know the details on future plans and aspirations. If the information is confidential, board members simply need to be told so. They are trusted advocates.

- *Being transparent about finances and the role of philanthropy.*
  Board members need to understand what the bottom line is,
  what sources are generating revenue, and how the bottom
  line is eroded by everything from contractual payments to
  self-pay patients. They need to know if the organization
  receives government money beyond payment for services
  from Medicaid and Medicare, and if so, where it comes
  from, what it is for, and whether it is adequate to address the
  need it is supposed to meet. Furthermore, board members
  should know the role philanthropy serves, how donor dollars
  are used, and the impact charitable giving has had on the
  organization. Giving board members the details on finance
  and philanthropy enables them to build understanding and
  partnerships in the community.
- *Preparing the board to be confident and effective ambassadors
  for giving.* Board members deserve coaching on the nuances
  of effectively engaging others and solidifying partnerships
  through solicitation. Whether this knowledge is shared through
  orientation, manuals, retreats, dedicated time in meetings,
  or other methods, board members are more confident as
  advocates and better prepared to advance the mission if they
  have understandable and reliable information about how to be
  effective in their role of connecting others to the organization.
  A balance is to be struck here, though: Board preparation
  is about being a coach and resource provider rather than a
  cheerless taskmaster. It is about enabling everyone to joyfully
  and collectively reach new heights.

SUCCESS IS A TEAM SPORT

Asking others to invest in the organization's future through philanthropy is a collective responsibility of the entire organization.
While board members joyfully bring their considerable leverage

to the table, many of these community volunteers also expect to see certain behaviors modeled in the healthcare organization to solidify their support.

Unfurling Leadership

Significant board member participation is often contingent on seeing organizational leaders model and advance philanthropy. For this reason, participation in healthcare philanthropy often unfolds from the inside out, starting with the healthcare organization CEO and senior executives, including the foundation executive. In this responsibility rests opportunity; healthcare leaders who demonstrate ownership help that behavior and interest spread to the rest of the organization. The importance of this lever is discussed in Chapter 6.

Affirming Governance

Philanthropy is primary to solidifying the strength and continuity of a healthcare organization's healing mission. Therefore, it is not a function to pass off to the foundation board, a development committee, or the foundation staff. In other words, the foundation board should not be the only body of community leaders engaged in fund development. The healthcare organization governing board has a fiduciary responsibility to ensure the long-term sustainability of the healthcare system as a community asset and safeguard its mission to provide quality patient care. Thus, it is incumbent on healthcare organization board leaders not only to evaluate the role and position of philanthropy in the organization's overall financial strategy but also to be actively engaged in cultivation and solicitation. While establishing a foundation board brings more mission-driven, community-oriented leaders to the task of advancing philanthropy, it does not replace the role of the healthcare organization board in actively engaging donor partners. If both boards do not work in concert in the fund development role, they place the organization at a distinct disadvantage.

Unleashing Potential

The quality of the relationship between the foundation board of directors and the foundation executive sets the tone, communication level, and engagement level for the entire fund development effort. While the foundation executive technically works on behalf of the foundation board of directors, the highest-functioning relationships are built on mutual respect and shoulder-to-shoulder collaboration that leverages individual strengths. The foundation executive must empower the foundation board of directors by communicating high-value opportunities for board engagement, ensuring the board is well-informed of priorities and plans, providing support services and materials as needed, facilitating education or training to enable board members to be highly successful in their roles, and fostering communication between the board and other parts of the healthcare organization.

IN SUMMARY

Engagement of community board members in fund development as a key part of their fiduciary responsibilities improves results and enriches their personal experience by meaningfully involving them in the core mission. Board members can embrace several roles along the continuum of the fund development process that reflect their strengths to enable greater performance, but no role has as much leverage as their active engagement in personal cultivation and solicitation for major gifts. To enable their success in this capacity, healthcare organizations and foundation executives must ensure board leaders have the tools they need to be effective and confident advocates for the mission.

FIVE STEPS TO CREATING A PLATFORM FOR PERFORMANCE

1. **Make key roles explicit.** People who are thoughtful enough to join the board of a charitable organization want to fulfill their role well. Be forthright about the expectations of board membership so potential members can decide if the board is a good match for them. If a board member is not willing to make the critical commitments of **engaging, giving,** and **connecting,** that person's involvement is a disservice to both the individual and the organization. Give candidates the information they need to make a sound decision.

2. **Give them the tools.** Few people wake up one day knowing how to solicit or understanding the need for philanthropy in healthcare. Give foundation and healthcare organization board members the tools they need to be successful. Schedule a board education session on philanthropy. Do a primer on healthcare finance. Invite physicians to provide clinical insights on the current case for support. In short, set the stage for excellence.

3. **Create actionable "cheat sheets."** Give board members talking points about current funding priorities, organization financials, and so forth to carry with them. The objective here is to enable members to be authoritative advocates, not to bury them in factoids. Narrow down the information to important points that fit on a single 3×5 index card.

4. **Engage the whole team.** Keep the healthcare organization board involved as essential members of the philanthropy team. Add a session on the rationale for philanthropy and meaningful ways to advance giving to new board member orientation, and

structure opportunities for communication and interaction between the healthcare and foundation boards.

5. **Get to 100 percent.** Adopt and proactively advance a plan to get to 100 percent board member giving at a level commensurate with each member's ability.

Interview with Scott H. Sikes, CFRE, FAHP, CFP, Vice President for Development and Community Relations and Executive Director, Shepherd Center (hospital) and Shepherd Center Foundation

Based in Atlanta, Georgia, Shepherd Center Foundation is a 501(c)(3) charitable organization supporting Shepherd Center, the nation's largest nonprofit hospital devoted to research, intensive and acute medical care, rehabilitation, and advocacy for people with spinal cord injury and disease, acquired brain injury, multiple sclerosis, and chronic pain (www.shepherd.org). Patients come to Shepherd Center from all 50 states and nearly 50 foreign countries.

QUESTION: How has Shepherd Center proactively engaged board members?

ANSWER: We utilize a system of four volunteer boards including: a board of directors, a foundation board of trustees, an advisory board, and an auxiliary board. My position serves as a communications/coordination point for all four boards. Before they begin service, all board members know they must be engaged in philanthropy through personal giving and fundraising. In new member orientation, we ask each board member to do four things in addition to attending their respective board's meetings: (1) make an annual gift, (2) attend and bring friends to at least one fundraising special event each year, (3) make an occasional major gift to a campaign, and (4) include us in their estate plans.

→

QUESTION: What specific activities, training, materials, or other support do you feel made an especially positive impact in enabling them to be successful?

ANSWER: Our culture of philanthropy comes from the very top of the organization and has permeated the organization from its earliest days. I am the only vice president who has a formal report at every meeting of the board of directors and each of the other boards. From the very top, this organization knows philanthropy is crucial to its daily efforts to serve patients and families.

QUESTION: How has board engagement enhanced philanthropy efforts?

ANSWER: We would not be here as an organization if it weren't for our boards.

QUESTION: If you had advice for healthcare CEOs on the importance of engaging board members in supporting philanthropy, what would it be?

ANSWER: The CEO must be personally committed to philanthropy through her or his own personal giving; must go on donor cultivation, solicitation, stewardship visits with trustees, volunteers, and/or staff; must cheerfully attend all major fundraising events; and each board meeting must have at least five minutes formally devoted to fundraising reports. All board members and the CEO must also have an expectation that fundraising is not done in a vacuum—that is, philanthropy must permeate an organization's culture. A culture of philanthropy only exists when the very top people are committed to philanthropy through their own visible giving, fundraising, and volunteering.

CHAPTER 4

Honoring the Expertise
of Physician Leaders

*It is more important to know what kind of person has the
disease than to know what kind of disease the person has.*

—*Hippocrates (460–377 BC)*

WHEN YOU ASK patients who was responsible for saving their
lives, most will name a physician. While many nurses, technicians,
therapists, and other experts may be part of the healthcare team
that influences or enables a patient's return to health, most patients
see physicians as the leaders who determine their outcomes.

The doctor–patient relationship is a cornerstone of American
medicine. Physicians historically have held an esteemed role in our
culture. The gravitas of a white coat signals authority and inspires
respect disproportionate to that accorded many other professionals. People often trust physicians implicitly and literally put their
lives in their hands.

The engagement of physicians in advancing the cause of healthcare philanthropy has an outsize effect, especially on efforts to
solicit grateful patients. Of affluent donors, 22 percent say a physician from the soliciting hospital would most influence their decision
to make a major gift, outnumbering those who say they would be
most influenced by the hospital CEO (13 percent). In the community hospital setting, those stating they would be most influenced

by a board member come in at a close second, at 21 percent (Bentz Whaley Flessner 2011).

ENGAGEMENT OF PHYSICIAN PARTNERS

The physician–patient relationship, while two-sided, has traditionally placed the balance of power and, in many cases, the ultimate prerogative for treatment decisions in the hands of the physician. Yet it has typically been a relationship built on trust and often on warmth. People do not forget the selflessness and dedication their doctor demonstrated when he rushed to the hospital in the middle of the night. They do not forget the compassion with which a difficult diagnosis was delivered. They do not forget the patience with which their physician explained her plan to navigate a complicated medical situation to enable a good outcome. For all the reasons that bind patients to their physicians, the physician can play a key, and sometimes critical and irreplaceable, role in fostering philanthropic support.

Acknowledging the "Cracks"

The discussion thus far is not suggesting there are no cracks in the relationship. Many forces can come between the doctor and patient. A July 2008 article in the *New York Times* goes so far as to boldly state "the once-revered doctor–patient relationship is on the rocks" (Parker-Pope 2008). The author contends that "[t]he reasons for all this frustration are complex. Doctors, facing declining reimbursements and higher costs, have only minutes to spend with each patient. News reports about medical errors and drug industry influence have increased patients' distrust" (Parker-Pope 2008). Newly empowered by access to a proliferation of medical information on the Internet, patients also have more opinions about their care, and the days of unquestioned compliance have likely passed.

In a recent *Good Morning America* report, physicians discussed patient frustration with extended wait times and whether doctors could rightfully be billed for this lost time (Conley 2011).

There are cracks in the façade of the doctor–healthcare organization relationship, too. Doctors no longer work within an institution's walls purely as partners; many are also independent-minded competitors. Furthermore, many physicians are on the medical staffs of several healthcare organizations—an arrangement that splits not only their time but also their loyalty.

Despite the challenges of doctor–patient and doctor–hospital relationships, physicians are still best positioned to make strong connections with grateful patients.

Optimized Roles for Physicians

While physicians are most influential at the front line in face-to-face interaction with prospective and current donors, they can play a variety of high-value roles in advancing philanthropy. These opportunities enable physicians to tailor their engagement to their individual strengths and mitigate any limitations or challenges. Potential activities include

- **sharing medical expertise** in their areas of specialty;
- **giving inspiring presentations** at events to educate and engage donors;
- **demonstrating technology** on behind-the-scenes tours;
- **sharing firsthand, personal stories** to show the impact of care;
- **identifying community members**—sometimes patients—interested in the organization;
- **engaging their physician peers** in the philanthropy effort, especially peers to whom they refer their patients;
- **explaining the role of giving** in community health presentations;

- **referring grateful patients** who express an interest in giving back to the organization;
- **making personal, face-to-face calls** on key prospects;
- **signing solicitation letters** to their peers and the community;
- **soliciting contributions from vendors** who service their offices or specialties;
- **providing or editing clinical information** in case statements;
- **displaying information about giving** in their private offices;
- **thanking donors** by showing them the clinical impact of giving; and
- **making a personal gift** that will motivate and inspire others.

Challenges to Engagement

Challenges to engaging physicians in philanthropy range from anxiety about being professionally appropriate to effective use of their time. Common issues include the following:

- **Concern about upholding HIPAA privacy rules:** The American Hospital Association, American Medical Association, and Association for Healthcare Philanthropy all have issued guidance on physician participation in cultivation and solicitation activities. A primary consideration has been how to engage patients in a manner that maintains their privacy. The bottom line is that physicians can take on an active role while maintaining HIPAA compliance.
- **Time limitations:** Despite long hours, physicians are pulled in so many directions that their time for other activities is limited. Physicians are also under pressure for efficient throughput and productivity in the patient care environment, so the time they have to spend on valued patients is already compressed. Physicians are also called on to support many other leadership and service roles in the healthcare organization. For all these reasons, it can be a challenge for a physician to find 90 minutes

to go on a solicitation call. Physician time—as the time of all allies—should be used judiciously for high-value, high-impact interactions at key times. Foundation offices can extend physician time by managing all the logistics of visits and other interactions—for example, by obtaining phone numbers, setting meetings, and driving or providing detailed directions. If physicians are assured their time is respected and are called on only for critical interactions, they are more likely to dedicate time.

- **Less ownership of hospital progress/more complexity in hospital–physician relationships:** As noted earlier, the physician–hospital relationship has changed. Many physicians spread their time between multiple facilities where they are on the active staff, leaving them with less ownership of/loyalty to the progress of any one healthcare organization. Other physicians compete with their hospitals, whether by performing more labs, tests, and minor procedures in their own offices or by having their own dedicated surgery centers. Still, physicians have a personal stake in enhancing the care environment; ultimately, they have some level of interest in ensuring the progress and innovation of the healthcare organization in which they provide care, for their own and their patients' sake.

- **Concerns about the professional ethics of soliciting patients:** Physicians are reluctant to potentially violate the sacred doctor–patient relationship. They are anxious that a request for a gift could be interpreted as a quid pro quo for the continuance of excellent care. Physicians may also fear that a patient who has been asked for a gift may be hesitant to return to them for care or call them if a crisis develops if that patient is not interested in making a gift. This sensitive territory must be navigated delicately and directly to establish the social mores of this relationship. As always, relationships should be founded on integrity, and the donor's interests and needs should always be primary. One way to deal with physicians' concern that patients will be reticent to call them after an appeal has been made is to clarify that the physician's role on the call is primarily that of an expert rather than an "asker," unless the physician is comfortable and willing to ask. In most situations, the physician shares the clinical vision, the impact it would have on patients, the implications for the caliber of medicine in the community, and so forth. Some physicians, however, are successful, well-received askers.

- **Fear of failure in the solicitation arena:** Physicians may be comfortable with a scalpel in their hand, but they may not be comfortable with a request for money coming out of their mouth. They are generally high-performing, highly driven individuals who are not accustomed to being put in situations in which they feel they could be set up for failure. However, because physicians are compelling and successful advocates, the development team needs to provide them with coaching and tools to enable them to confidently advance the development endeavor, including
  —information on appropriate involvement under HIPAA,
  —talking points on project highlights and frequent questions,
  —information on how to handle potential objections,
  —referral forms they can use to capture contact information from grateful patients who wish to give, and
  —solicitation training and participation in mock solicitation exercises.

Development organizations also need to take the fear out of dealing with the foundation. Some physicians fear that a fund development professional will walk into a patient's room to ask for money or do something equally egregious that will disrespect the patient or the doctor–patient relationship. Therefore, the role and intent of the foundation need to be transparent. Physicians should be told in advance how the development organization handles specific situations and what its overall intent is. Physicians need to feel assured that the work is undergirded by integrity to place their trust in the foundation as a positive force for good.

IDENTIFYING POTENTIAL ALLIES

The aim is not to engage every physician in the organization. The goal is to engage those who are best positioned to be compelling and trusted advocates in advancing the image of and community's attachment to the healthcare organization's mission. Physicians suited for the advocate role have the following qualities:

- They are respected by both their peers and the greater community.
- They are passionate advocates for both their specialty and the institution at large.
- They are considered thought leaders and opinion shapers.
- They are able to translate the jargon of medicine into understandable terms.
- They have a warm, positive communication style.
- They are willing to make a personal financial investment in the mission.

The healthcare organization CEO and chief medical officer are important allies in establishing rapport, creating trust, and facilitating access to engage physicians on a broader scale. However, physicians can also be engaged on a case-by-case basis as new strategic focus areas for the healthcare organization and related funding priorities emerge. Many organizations induce physician involvement in philanthropy by making the prioritization of a project for philanthropic funding contingent on the availability and willingness of physicians in the project-related specialty to serve.

Cultivating Physician Interest

To convince physicians to be part of philanthropy endeavors—as either askers or givers—the development organization has to explain what is in it for them and for the patients they serve.

Physicians need to see they have a vested interest in the success and advancement of the healthcare organization. It even behooves independent contractors to be part of the process of identifying and securing charitable resources to fuel progress in the care environment and acquire the technology and support they need to do their work well. In an era of limited resources, their involvement enables clinical leadership and innovation in the organization where they practice and may literally determine whether or not they get what is on their wish lists. Altruistic purposes also are at stake; participation in the noble role of advancing giving helps secure the health of the greater community.

By extension, one cannot assume that a physician will give just because he or she is a physician. Like any other donor, the development organization must find a match between the physician's values and priorities and those of the healthcare organization. For example, one likely would not ask a female donor with a history of heart trouble to provide a gift to a campaign for prostate cancer. In the same way, cardiac physicians would be less motivated to support projects outside their specialty, their specialty's associated referral patterns, or their personal interests. Unless the organization

---

Keeping Giving Top of Mind

Consistent communication with physicians about the role and current use of philanthropy helps them see it in context. A variety of tools can be used for this task:

- Articles in existing medical staff newsletters
- Medical staff and section meetings
- Signage in the physician lounge
- Signage by the exit to the physician parking lot
- Collateral tailored to the needs and interests of physicians
- Recognition programs exclusively for physician donors

---

is the only healthcare facility in town or unless most of the physicians in the area are employed by the healthcare organization, an objective of securing a gift from every member of the medical staff is unrealistic. Instead, the ambition should be to secure the involvement and investment of those who are true believers in the institution, those for whom the facility is their primary place of practice, and those who see how their future and the organization's future are tied together.

HONOR THE COMMITMENT

Physicians who are willing to step up and participate in philanthropy play a valuable role only they can fulfill. Just as donors should not be seen as checkbooks, key allies should not feel they are just an extra set of hands. As with any ally, it is valuable to thank physicians for taking on the responsibility of being an advocate. This recognition is especially meaningful when given in front of their physician peers or the organization's community board members. To further honor their commitment, the development foundation might offer physicians opportunities for involvement beyond solicitation, such as the following:

- **Serving on the foundation board:** Key allies or potential allies can be positioned on the foundation board to immerse them in the charitable aspect of the hospital's mission and to see the work from the inside. This opportunity lends power to their voice when they share their confidence in how the work is conducted—especially when speaking to their peers.
- **Identifying opportunities:** Physicians can be given a voice and a role in identifying new opportunities, setting funding priorities, shaping plans, and so forth. While this involvement needs to be structured outside hospital politics, there is no better way to foster physician engagement.

- **Shaping messages:** Physicians can be invited to help shape the case for support for key projects in their areas, including enunciating the clinical case, business case, and mission case.

IN SUMMARY

Physicians provide unique value to the development process by sharing clinical expertise and engaging grateful patients. To advance philanthropy efforts, development organizations should seek to involve physicians who share a passion for the mission, are respected by their peers and the community, and are compelling advocates. Ultimately, physician involvement in giving not only benefits the community but also enables the innovation and clinical leadership physicians need to provide high-quality care to their patients.

THREE STEPS TO CREATING A PLATFORM FOR PERFORMANCE

1. **Overcome obstacles.** Address the issues of HIPAA and ethical professional behavior head-on by acknowledging the potential concern and sharing specific information about how physicians can be appropriately involved in philanthropy.
2. **Provide tools.** Offer training sessions or create support materials specific to physician involvement in philanthropy. Share opportunities for leveraging physician involvement. Walk through or provide examples of potential scripting with grateful patients. Show physicians how to tell powerful mission stories.
3. **Induce physician involvement.** Insist that any project considered for philanthropic funding have a physician champion. Physicians who see their peers' services benefitting from their active involvement in philanthropy may be inspired to step up in turn.

Interview with J. William Kinard, Jr., FAHP, CFRE,
Director of Philanthropy, Greenville Hospital System
Children's Hospital, Greenville, South Carolina

Greenville Hospital System (GHS) is a 1,100-bed not-for-profit academic medical center in Greenville, South Carolina. The system has 7,500 employees and 1,000 members on the medical staff. GHS is affiliated with the Medical University of South Carolina and the University of South Carolina medical schools. The system's five campuses include community hospitals, a long-term acute-care hospital, a nursing home, outpatient facilities, and wellness centers.

QUESTION: How has your healthcare organization sought to proactively engage physicians in philanthropy?

ANSWER: As a physician-led organization, we took to heart the data found in the Bentz Whaley Flessner annual survey on "What the Affluent Say About Giving to Healthcare." For the entire ten-year span of these reports, the physician has ranked at the top among those whom the affluent regard as an influencer within the organization in their decision to give. Realizing the vital role his physician leaders play, the chairman of Pediatrics has made it clear that physician engagement in philanthropy is an expectation for any leader. With his expectation made clear, his request of philanthropy was then to "only work with those physicians who want to work with you." Once gifts began to come in the seven-figure range for engaged physicians, the engagement factor became contagious.

→

QUESTION: What specific messaging, activities, or materials do you feel made an especially positive impact in fostering physician engagement?

ANSWER: We developed a protocol that we refer to as the "Eight-Point Plan for Resource Development." We found physician leaders who are engaged with us to be very pleased with a protocol. One physician has said to me that—and I'll paraphrase—all physicians are creatures of protocol. It is how we are trained. The Eight-Point Plan makes our work/role easy to understand.

We don't put the physician in the role of "asking for money." Much more importantly, we place them as the principal influencer along with a strong community champion (board member, donor, parent, etc.) with the principal focus of referring and developing relationships.

The Plan covers all aspects of the resource development process from uncovering the "Dream Gap," a financial analysis of the cost (with input from Operations), formal approval with signatures for the concept, writing the case, formal orientation of physician and community champions, preparing those whose story is the core of the new case, and establishing a series of highly selective and strategic connection points with those having the capacity and affinity to help us.

Finally, we measure this movement with a metrics system that we have developed that only measures "what matters" in the Resource Development Plan. There is also a file that has been developed which contains all of this activity in one electronic record. It is much like an electronic patient record. This way, the physician and I will be able to see the case's file each time we visit.

→

QUESTION: How do you feel the engagement of physicians has enhanced your efforts to advance philanthropy?

ANSWER: We are very fortunate in that pediatricians seem to possess a more natural propensity, if not even perspicacity, toward the Relationship Development Plan. Another key data point in the BWF survey is that 69 percent of the affluent indicate that the attribute most appealing to them in an "influencer" is knowledge of the case/organization. Who better to fill this role than physicians? As they feel it is a more natural role, they are then by default more comfortable.

QUESTION: If you had advice for healthcare CEOs on the importance of physician engagement in supporting vibrant philanthropy, what would it be?

ANSWER:

1. Create an environment where physicians know that to be a leader they must be engaged in resource development. It is the remaining great frontier for their dreams for clinical, research, and teaching aspirations. Few health systems have the available cash on hand as we did in the previous two decades to fund every truly innovative idea and process improvement. Today's physician leader is one who understands that no matter her "place" in the organization, cash doesn't appear because she can press the administration. Reform and shrinking margins require her to know how to excel in the resource development process. It is the role of Institutional Advancement to assist physicians in what I believe to be yet another fellowship in resource development.

2. The affluent indicate, by double-digit percentages, that their influencers are physician champions, community champions, and CEOs. Far behind these and in single-digit levels are the development officer and the

→

CDO. That begs us to better understand the role of advancement professionals as that of the conduit that ties the prospective donor to the influencers. We do this by creating a strong protocol for success and orienting the influencers toward excellence in this role. It is our job to teach, to evaluate, and [to] facilitate. CEOs who rely on advancement professionals to "go get it" are committing themselves to a culture of poor performance and far less available cash on hand to meet ever-increasing needs for program growth, sustainability brought about by endowment building, and far fewer, less committed donors and prospects.

3. Realize that the CEO has, now more than ever, an incumbent role to play in the Resource Development Plan. The affluent have labeled them as an influencer. They have been called into the game! Embrace the role, know the Eight-Point Plan, and work with advancement professionals to rise to the challenge. CEOs of tomorrow will not have the mind-set that the foundation should just go get what [they] need.

QUESTION: What else do we need to know?

ANSWER:

1. Your physicians are your best fundraisers. Give them the tools and advancement professionals who understand how to help them.

2. Over one-third of the affluent who have made major gifts cite a personal or family clinical experience as their motivation to give. Physicians are your best prospect generators. Empower them with a HIPAA-appropriate referral mechanism that is not arduous and respects their relationship with the patient/family.

3. It is fun . . . embrace it . . . challenge the culture . . . make a difference.

CHAPTER 5

Empowering the Chief Development Officer

*They will be able to manage, inspire, evaluate,
communicate, anticipate, listen, articulate the mission,
and engage others—particularly donors—
in the purpose and plans of the organization.*

—Kay Sprinkel Grace, philanthropy consultant

THE ROLE OF THE CHIEF DEVELOPMENT OFFICER

The chief development officer (CDO) serves as a catalyst, communicator, cheerleader, constant, and connector in fund development efforts.

- As a **catalyst**, the CDO functions as an internal consultant who designs strategy, directs the execution of the development plans, ensures integration of related but different development programs, and evaluates each program as well as the comprehensive development enterprise.
- As a **communicator**, the CDO shapes a case for support that will engage and inspire others to help advance the mission of the organization and ensures consistency of voice and messaging across a variety of communication channels.
- As a **cheerleader**, the CDO engages and enables an array of key allies from board members to executives, trains and

mentors development staff, and rallies the entire team of allies and staff to advance charitable giving.

- As a **constant**, the CDO ensures the continuity and smooth progression of development initiatives as board leaders and board members change.
- As a **connector**, the CDO functions as a bridge between the healthcare organization and the community and between the healthcare organization and its affiliated charitable organization.

The CDO is a primary ambassador of the healthcare organization and, of all the hospital's leaders, the executive with whom a donor communicates most consistently. To effectively position and advocate the work of the organization, CDOs must be "highly informed and capable institutional insiders" (Hodson 2010). They need to be well-informed about not only fund development practices but also the strategy, operations, and finances of the healthcare facility so they can confidently and accurately articulate the organization's case for support and its compelling vision for the future. Thus, the savvy healthcare organization ensures the CDO is included in relevant forums to glean information appropriate for sharing with key constituencies and to build relationships with board members and other organizational leaders.

The CDO brings the perspective of the community into the healthcare organization. As an executive with a strong external focus, he or she spends a disproportionate amount of time outside the organization, often with key community, business, civic, and social leaders. In general, the CDO is also the only organizational leader besides the CEO who has a reporting relationship to a community board of directors. Thus, the CDO is well positioned to relate questions and concerns from the community to the organization and to share the organization's perspective with the community. The organization needs to prepare the CDO to hear, process, and respond to issues that may be bubbling in the public consciousness. A CDO who communicates effectively keeps community thought leaders engaged and informed in an ongoing, substantive dialogue with the organization.

The CDO facilitates high-value, leveraged interactions between organizational allies and key donors and prospects. Rather than have "all hands on deck" at all times, he or she ensures the CEO, senior executives, board members, and physicians are prepared for key interactions at key times to advance donor relationships. The CDO also ensures that the development team provides the organization's allies with relevant donor history, research, case information, and proposals to enable them to have informed interactions with current and prospective donor partners. He or she often serves as an "architect" on solicitation calls by being fully versed not only in the case for support but also in important details, such as the types of gifts the organization accepts, pledge periods, payment plans, and recognition opportunities.

Finally, the CDO is an "internal development consultant." He or she stays apprised of changes and trends in fund development practices, current legislation, and economic factors—both general and healthcare related—that affect giving and translates this information to others.

ENABLING THE SUCCESS OF THE CHIEF DEVELOPMENT OFFICER

Due to the public nature of the CDO role and the need to integrate it into the healthcare organization at the highest levels, the CDO usually reports to the CEO of the healthcare organization. However, many CDOs have dual reporting relationships to the healthcare organization's CEO and to the foundation organization's board of directors. To ensure this arrangement works smoothly, organizations should affirm the duties and responsibilities of the CDO and the expectations of hospital administration and the governing board in advance. A key issue to address is authority: delineating who singly or collectively retains the power to hire, evaluate, promote, and dismiss.

The healthcare organization can take proactive steps to position the CDO for success. Because job titles confer external credibility and internal access, most CDOs are vice presidents or senior vice presidents of the healthcare organization and sit on the executive team. The department/discipline they oversee as vice president might be called "development," "advancement," "philanthropy," "community partnerships," or some other name. Many CDOs also are president or CEO of the separate foundation organization. By assigning the CDO a senior officer-level title, the organization signals to donors that this person represents the organization and is authorized to negotiate on its behalf. Having a senior title also helps the CDO secure appointments with key community leaders, many of whom have similar titles. Inside the organization, a senior title opens opportunities to participate in forums and lends credibility in interactions with the healthcare organization's board and other members of its leadership team.

THE IDEAL CHIEF DEVELOPMENT OFFICER

What qualities make a person an ideal fit for the CDO position? Colette Murray (2011), president of the nonprofit executive search firm Paschal Murray, shares, "Always, always, always, integrity is the number one quality you must have. Then, for positions anywhere from an MGO [major gifts officer] to a CDO, they would need to have a track record of actually being involved in major gifts work focused on relationships and cultivation and solicitation. Finally, it would be someone who has been involved in facilitating the involvement of the CEO and boards. Basically, you want to find someone who has clear commitment to integrity who has also really walked the walk." Another intrinsic quality to seek is genuine passion for the healthcare mission. The candidate must have a fundamental interest in and appreciation for healthcare to convey the needs and opportunities of the healthcare organization to others convincingly.

Because the CDO is a visible community role and a primary contact for many key stakeholders, community leaders, and hospital and foundation board members, the position demands someone with poise, discretion, and an ability to deftly communicate the importance of the healthcare organization's work, both orally and in writing. A solid development leader also has the management skills required to execute strategy, evaluate results, and successfully lead and inspire the development team. The talents needed in a CDO depend on where the development organization is in its life cycle; builders are often different from sustainers. Candidates should be evaluated for organizational fit in this regard

---

Basic Qualities and Characteristics to Seek in a Chief Development Officer

- Unquestionable integrity
- Success in previous development roles
- Passion for the healthcare cause
- Compelling and articulate communication style
- Inspirational motivator, teacher, coach, and mentor
- Warm and genuine approach to building relationships
- Active listener
- Physical and emotional energy
- Proactive personality and drive
- Authentic and credible presence
- Positive and gracious attitude in "defeat"
- Vision to see the big picture and capture emerging opportunities
- Skilled manager and planner
- Discretion and duty of confidentiality
- Ability to juggle disparate tasks

---

and in terms of organizational culture. Finally, Jim Collins beautifully sums up the desirable work ethic of a nonprofit executive in his monograph *Good to Great and the Social Sectors:* Organizations need to seek "those who are productively neurotic, those who are self-motivated and self-disciplined, those who wake up every day, compulsively driven to do the best they can because it is simply part of their DNA" (Collins 2005).

Chief Development Officer Job Description

Courtesy of Paschal Murray Executive Search

Executive Vice President/Chief Development Officer

Reports to: President/CEO

The Chief Development Officer (CDO)/Executive Vice President (EVP) provides overall fundraising leadership for HEALTHCARE ORGANIZATION and administrative responsibility for HEALTHCARE FOUNDATION.

As chief fundraising officer for the FOUNDATION, the CDO/EVP is responsible for planning, directing and evaluating all aspects of the Foundation including: major, planned and endowment giving, annual giving, capital campaigns, community benefits, corporate grants program and donor recognition.

The CDO/EVP manages a focused and strategic approach to fundraising initiatives with priority projects set by HEALTHCARE ORGANIZATION CEO.

The ideal candidate would develop relationships at all levels in the organization and maintain others' confidence through character and competence.

$\rightarrow$

Primary descriptive roles of the CDO/ EVP include:

- External and Internal Influencer
- Strategist and Function Leader
- Results Driven
- Change Sponsor

The CDO/EVP must be comfortable in both a relationship-oriented and performance-based culture; promotes a culture that is transparent; has a servant leadership philosophy; builds consensus and is decisive when appropriate and takes calculated risks; operates with a certain sense of both humility and resolve.

1. Philanthropic Development
   Provide overall leadership and strategic direction managing all operational aspects of philanthropic development for FOUNDATION.

2. Foundation Board
   Identify and cultivate Foundation board members and foster their growth and involvement with the Foundation; facilitate and lead quarterly board meetings; lead and direct Foundation board committees and provide oversight direction to board committees.

3. Financial Accountability
   Accountable for all Foundation contributions to include: Proper disposition of all donor contributions; fiscal responsibility for all appropriations; administration of restricted and endowed funds; oversee audit and compliance issues; monitor and evaluate Foundation financial performance; serve as a liaison to Foundation's asset manager; serve as primary agent in contracts and agreements relative to Foundation business.

→

4. Donor and Community Responsibilities
   Directly responsible for organizational fundraising;
   serves as intermediary to philanthropic community;
   actively participates in cultivation and solicitation of
   major gifts; maintains relationships with contributors,
   board members of multiple boards, medical staff and
   community leaders; communicates HEALTHCARE
   ORGANIZATION mission and needs to community.

5. Hospital Responsibilities
   Participate in the overall executive leadership of
   HEALTHCARE ORGANIZATION and provide leadership
   and counsel on issues related to philanthropy.

Qualities and experiences ideal candidates should display
include:

- Baccalaureate degree from a four-year college or university.
- Ten years' experience as a fundraising professional.
- Five years successful experience in a fundraising
  leadership capacity.
- Proven major gifts and development program expertise
  and insights.
- Experience leading development initiatives achieving
  noteworthy results.
- Proven track record in a competitive philanthropic
  community.
- Experience building/managing sophisticated professional
  & support staff.
- Experience managing important major gift relationships.
- Track record of building engaging partnerships with
  significant donors and maintaining community and
  corporate partnerships.

$\rightarrow$

- Ability to influence multiple levels from board to major gift donors to employees to community and political leaders.
- Ability to build trusted interpersonal relationships that create confidence.
- Familiarity with health care products and services.

Preference will be given to candidates [who] also display one or more of the following:

- An advanced academic degree.
- Professional fundraising certification (CFRE or FAHP).

Source: Paschal Murray (2012). Used with permission.

The field of fund development has become increasingly professionalized, raising the standards for those who aspire to serve as CDO. Many development leaders now have professional certifications. To achieve the Certified Fund Raising Executive (CFRE) designation, individuals must have five years of successful experience in fundraising and pass a written exam. Individuals with ten years of professional experience in development are eligible to pursue the Fellow of the Association for Healthcare Philanthropy (FAHP) credential, which is awarded upon successful completion of written and oral examinations. Academic programs in fund development were available as early as 1959 when Columbia University started a master's program on the subject. Today, undergraduate and graduate programs are available on both nonprofit management and philanthropy; Indiana University Center on Philanthropy conferred the world's first doctorate in philanthropic studies in 2008 (Sargeant and Shang 2010, 41). However, at this time, most senior development officers do not have degrees specific to their philanthropy or nonprofit management function because such programs did not proliferate until the 1990s.

Finding and Keeping

Finding and retaining a CDO can be challenging. The continued expansion of the nonprofit sector and increased prioritization of fund development activities in healthcare and other sectors have led to shorter tenures and more movement among all ranks of development professionals. Seasoned development officers are in shorter supply, change jobs more often, and are more selective about the roles they accept.

Organizations can find and retain excellent development talent if the right environment and conditions are in place. CDOs

---

What Are Chief Development Officers Looking For?

- A mission that inspires passion
- A savvy CEO who understands the value of philanthropy
- A direct reporting relationship and steady communication with, and routine access to, the CEO
- A clear and compelling strategic vision
- Strategically aligned charitable projects
- Engagement of the hospital and foundation boards in the development effort
- Positioning in the organization that enables access to information and allies
- A development budget and infrastructure conducive to success
- A positive relationship between the healthcare organization and the community
- An organization that has a reputation for integrity
- A senior executive title that conveys credibility and facilitates access
- Ability to participate in professional groups and continuing education

---

seek to work with leaders who nurture philanthropy and involve them in fulfilling work. A mission with genuine merit is nonnegotiable; CDOs need to feel they can authentically and passionately advocate it in the community. They also want to work under the direct leadership of a CEO they respect and with whom they see potential for close collaboration. While other aspects of the environment are highly desirable, such as a board that is already engaged in development work or a culture of philanthropy, those elements can take root in the organization under the direction of an inspired CDO who has the support of a committed CEO.

An appropriate, regionally and nationally competitive salary has also become more important. Nonprofit organizations must pay competitively enough to attract talent but not handsomely enough to attract criticism. The Association for Healthcare Philanthropy (www.ahp.org) regularly conducts an authoritative salary study broken down by title, region of service, years of experience, and other criteria. Other professional fund development organizations, such as the Association of Fundraising Professionals (www.afpnet.org), also conduct regular salary studies on professionals working for a variety of causes, from health to arts to education. Nonprofit healthcare and university fundraising professionals typically receive more competitive salaries than do those in other sectors because of the depth, breadth, and complexity of their programs, so an organization seeking to benchmark CDO compensation should compare salaries from hospital to hospital or hospital to local university rather than from hospital to local social service organization or national health organization chapter office in the organization's service area. Ultimately, organizations should determine salaries that attract the level of talent they need and deter loss of talent to other foundations.

The code of professional ethics to which most fund development professionals subscribe bars percentage compensation and sets clear rules for other financial incentives. Under the ethical provisions of the Association for Healthcare Philanthropy, the Association of Fundraising Professionals, and other leading fund development groups, CDO compensation based on funds raised is considered inappropriate because the best interests of donors should come before the self-interest of the development professional. Ethical, appropriate ways to attract, incentivize, recognize, and retain key fund development professionals include offering professionally oriented benefits, such as continuing professional education; reimbursement of CFRE and FAHP examination fees; and memberships to professional organizations, such as the Association for Healthcare Philanthropy, American College of Healthcare Executives, Association of Fundraising Professionals, Advisory Board Company Philanthropy Leadership Council, and Partnership for Philanthropic Planning. These memberships provide structured opportunities to connect with industry peers, keep up with current practices, and stay abreast of legislation and other environmental factors affecting the industry. Benefits of this nature simultaneously reward performance, increase retention, and advance the professionalism of the staff. Development staff may also participate in organization-wide incentive programs as long as the triggers are defined in advance and are not related to dollars raised.

Structuring Appropriate Incentive Compensation

Professional fund development associations provide guidance on a variety of issues to ensure ethical practice. One of the knottier issues has been the appropriate use and structuring of incentive compensation programs to provide performance-based bonuses or supplements to a development professional's base salary. The guidelines' intent is to ensure the rights and respectful treatment of donors.

Development staff may not ethically accept incentive compensation based entirely or partially on a percentage

→

---

of charitable contributions raised. The rationale is that doing so violates the intent and trust of the donor because

- donors give to advance the mission of the healthcare organization, so if the donor knew the development professional were personally benefitting commensurately to the value of a gift, a trusting relationship between the two would be difficult to establish; and
- compensation based on a percentage of dollars raised could predispose development professionals to put their personal interests before donors' best interests.

Incentive compensation **is appropriate** when the following conditions are met:

- Incentives are based on the achievement of mutual, preestablished goals related to overall responsibilities and performance. Many organizations consider nonfinancial metrics, such as the number of new donors acquired.
- Incentive compensation is a norm throughout the healthcare organization.
- The incentive program is guided by a policy approved by the governing board.

Ethical compensation guidelines are also intended to ensure development professionals' compensation is based on their experience and effort rather than contingent on dollars raised. The Association for Healthcare Philanthropy and the Association of Fundraising Professionals conduct routine studies on market compensation rates for fund development professionals.

For more information on appropriate incentive compensation, visit www.afpnet.org.

Source: Adapted from Association of Fundraising Professionals (2009).

The implications of losing key staff extend beyond an unwanted vacancy and the need to recruit a new development leader; the organization also suffers from lost or delayed gifts attributable to key relationships that have been broken or transferred and need to be rebuilt. Organizations may find it more cost-effective to increase a high-performing development officer's salary or award the officer an allowable bonus to secure his or her continued service than to spend resources on recruiting, wait for the new hire to gain credibility and donors' trust, and rebuild donor relationships. However, the reasons development officers resign generally have little or nothing to do with compensation, so the most successful strategy may simply be to nurture a positive work environment. When asked why good development officers resign, Murray (2011) said, "Across the board, it is because the lack of relationship between the CDO and their immediate supervisor—so usually between the CDO and CEO, but sometimes between CDO and board. Keeping these relationships where they need to be is about communication, staying on the same page about goals, and sharing realistic expectations."

The Search for the Chief Development Officer

An Interview with Colette M. Murray, JD, President and CEO, Paschal Murray

Founded in 1978, Paschal Murray is an executive search firm specializing in hiring for fund development and nonprofit management.

QUESTION: Who should be involved in the CDO interview process?

ANSWER: Ideally interviews need to be done with a search committee that includes all those who need to be engaged

→

and have ownership for the final decision. The hospital really needs to decide who those people are in their environment and culture. Then, all finalists need to meet with the immediate supervisor—who is usually the CEO—with members of the development staff the CDO would inherit and with the board of directors.

QUESTION: What advice would you give to a healthcare CEO considering hiring a CDO?

ANSWER: CEOs need to understand this is an important search for a critical role, so we would encourage them to use an executive search firm. Further, the search firm they select should be one that specializes in development—which is probably not the one they have typically used for general leadership positions or for recruiting doctors. If you hire a firm focused on hiring fund development leaders, they have the advantage of being at philanthropy conferences and seeing the rising stars. It would be advisable to look at the membership of the Network of Nonprofit Search Consultants at www.nnsc.org to find a firm that specializes in finding nonprofit leaders.

QUESTION: What is the average time required to complete a successful search?

ANSWER: The minimum would be three months to about five months max. A search should not go past six months, or you will lose candidates. You tend to lose your best candidates who have other options if you drag your feet, since it is human nature that people tend to look at others, too, to see what their options are. That means you would ideally want to have six to eight weeks of seeking candidates. Then, once people are excited, you keep the process moving.

IN SUMMARY

CDOs are charged with building important community partnerships that will advance philanthropy. They are key, frontline executives who must be selected carefully on the basis of their potential to excel and cultural fit. The CDO must relate well with the CEO, the organization board, and the foundation board to be able to engage, inspire, and deploy key allies to advance the mission of the healthcare organization.

FOUR STEPS TO CREATING A PLATFORM FOR PERFORMANCE

1. **Hire right.** Seek someone with integrity, passion, great communication skills, a strong work ethic, and an ability to build strong and genuine relationships. This person will be a key ambassador for the organization in the community, so it is worth taking the time to hire well.
2. **Position correctly.** The CDO role should report to the CEO of the organization. Any other arrangement positions the function incorrectly and compromises its potential.
3. **Title well.** Assignment of a senior title that lends credibility and facilitates access is a simple but significant way of empowering the CDO. Many CDOs are vice presidents or senior vice presidents of the healthcare organization, president/CEO of the foundation, or both.
4. **Strategically locate.** Placement of the CDO's office in proximity to the offices of the CEO and other senior leaders breeds ongoing communication and enables easy drop-ins from key donors when such visits have the potential to add value.

Interview with Peter S. Fine, FACHE, President and CEO, Banner Health

Phoenix-based Banner Health is one of the largest nonprofit healthcare systems in the country. The system owns or manages 23 acute-care hospitals, long-term care centers, outpatient surgery centers, and an array of other services in seven states: Alaska, Arizona, California, Colorado, Nebraska, Nevada, and Wyoming.

QUESTION: What are the most important qualities in a foundation leader?

ANSWER: In our case, the position of chief development officer is held by the president and chief executive officer of Banner Health Foundation. Many qualities I believe are essential in such a role are not unlike the qualities I look for in every member of my senior management team. Not surprisingly, first and foremost is the ability to lead, both within the organization and throughout the community. Successful leaders understand how to gain trust by being highly visible and using their leadership influence to build lasting relationships and create collaborative opportunities.

While a background in healthcare might be helpful, it isn't essential. More important is the credibility of the chief development officer within both the philanthropic and business community. That credibility outside of the organization is necessary to entice the right people to serve on the foundation board of directors and in other leadership roles. Then, those trusting relationships can open doors to an entire network of key community members.

$\rightarrow$

One of the primary reasons Banner Health is recognized as a leader in our industry is due to the financial stability of the organization. While fundraising organizations require a somewhat different business model—one in which spending money to make money isn't uncommon—it is still essential to me that Banner Health Foundation operate in the same fiscally responsible manner as Banner Health. As such, I sought out a candidate who showed business savvy and the ability to do more with less and find cost-saving opportunities.

Any successful chief development officer must know their community. He or she must have a strong grasp of what people care about and what will motivate them to choose to give their discretionary income to your organization. Finally, equally important to every other attribute is a sincere sense of gratitude and appreciation and expertise in knowing an appropriate way to thank every donor.

QUESTION: How have you positioned the foundation CEO for success?

ANSWER: Part of my responsibility as president and CEO is to build a culture of philanthropy within Banner Health. Not only do we have a young foundation, but Banner Health is just 12 years old. We have ambitious goals and an aggressive strategic plan, and philanthropy will play a key role in our success.

My management team and I must be able to articulate the role and value of philanthropy. I've worked closely with the president and CEO of the foundation to build trust among the members of the leadership team. We must be able to work together and understand how our efforts support and benefit one another.

→

In every facet of our business, Banner Health is about measurable outcomes. To fulfill our mission, we need philanthropy. For every dollar the foundation raises, one of our hospitals would have to generate $20 in revenue to have a dollar left to invest. Conveying that value proposition to Banner leadership has helped bridge the gap between the work of the foundation and that of our hospitals.

As we have achieved various milestones or secured significant gifts, taking time to share those "wins" with Banner leadership has also been an important part of ensuring the success of the foundation and its president and CEO.

QUESTION: How do you and the foundation CEO enable each other?

ANSWER: The president and CEO of the foundation and I have developed a great working relationship and a good understanding about when to include me in donor cultivation efforts and what I can bring to those meetings. While I provide the business and healthcare perspective of Banner Health and speak to the things that make Banner one of the top healthcare systems in the nation, the foundation president and CEO balances that with humility, personal stories, and knowing exactly the right way to "make the ask" and recognize each donor.

QUESTION: What advice would you give to a healthcare CEO who is considering starting or repositioning a foundation?

ANSWER: First, the person you hire does matter. Take time to involve your board of directors in the selection process, and make sure the board understands your vision for the foundation and the role the chief development officer plays.

→

Also, it is critical to ensure your branding, marketing, and public relations team is on board and understands how the corporate side of healthcare and the foundation side must work together to be successful. Philanthropic communications and messaging often [have] a very different look and feel than traditional healthcare communications, but it is essential for efforts to align.

Most important, don't expect instant success. Dollars won't start flowing through the doors overnight. As CEO, you have to be willing to roll up your sleeves and work side by side with your chief development officer and be open to learning from one another.

PART III

Levers That Inspire Philanthropy

CHAPTER 6

Nurturing a Culture
of Philanthropy

*Notable differences exist between organizations that
achieve success in fundraising and those that do not.
But, the primary and most obvious difference is the
presence of, or lack of, a Philanthropic Culture.*

—*Karla A. Williams, philanthropy consultant*

ORGANIZATIONAL CULTURE IS like the wind; it is invisible, but
its effects can be seen and felt. Culture permeates all activities in a
healthcare organization. It is the sum of the attitudes, beliefs, actions,
motivations, and values of the people who make up the organization
and is a reflection of the way the organization deploys its mission.
It is the unspoken element that often unconsciously drives decision
making and is manifested individually and collectively in the way
staff members relate to each other and respond to the circumstances
they face. Simply, culture is the way things get done.

It is important to position the philanthropy endeavor in the
minds of executives, boards, physicians, and frontline staff as an
important, strategic lever the organization can use to advance its
highest objectives and ideals. Otherwise, the foundation may be
perceived as a decorative, social function run by glad-handers rather
than as a high-level, strategic function staffed by leaders who facilitate high-value community partnerships.

Culture is especially powerful and important in philanthropy because giving is fundamentally about relationships between those who make up the organization and the community. The more individuals an organization engages in enunciating the value of philanthropy and fostering meaningful relationships with patients and members of the community, the more connections the organization will have. The aim is not to create a swarm of solicitors but rather a chorus of believers.

If philanthropy is to become a cornerstone of organizational advancement, all staff need to be deployed to the task. Management guru Tom Peters (2007) said:

> The most important asset in every company is the esprit de corps: the motivation and passion of each employee . . . and . . . their willingness to collaborate together on whatever strategic projects are critical for growth. . . . A beautifully crafted strategy can fail when the employees in various divisions within an organization clash. Logically, we think that strategy should drive behavior, but, in reality, it's the culture—underlying norms, values, belief systems—that dictates how effectively people work together. . . . If strategy and culture are not aligned, the culture may support behaviors that conflict with what has to get done—and actually block execution of the strategy.

In short, if the organization as a whole has not bought into a culture that supports and extends philanthropy, its capacity for success is limited and a valuable opportunity for optimization is lost.

WHAT DOES A CULTURE OF PHILANTHROPY LOOK LIKE?

In a culture of philanthropy, the power and importance of giving are infused into daily organizational life at all levels and in all areas. It positions the act of inviting donors to support the healing mission as a noble endeavor to be embraced from the front line to the boardroom. A culture of philanthropy creates a common understanding of how community giving strengthens and sustains the organization. Everyone—regardless of role—is a champion for the organization and knows where to direct someone who expresses a willingness or desire to help. Members of the culture also recognize that their organization has the heart, soul, and legal status of any nonprofit organization that merits community support. They understand that **anyone** can make a difference by giving at whatever level he or she is able to, and they have a responsibility to be role models and give at whatever level is appropriate for their circumstances and inclination. In short, a culture of philanthropy has many facets. These common understandings are explored in the sections ahead.

Giving Is Accessible

Philanthropy is a big, inaccessible-sounding word. For some people, it smacks of "high society" or wealth. However, philanthropy is not about wealth or privilege; it is the heart—even the lifeblood—of the charitable healthcare organization. It is essential to boil down the word to make it a concept everyone can understand, embrace, and support. All can give, share, and care, whether they are able to share a lot or a "widow's mite": a meaningful gift that, while small, is commensurate with their means.

A healthcare organization should define philanthropy in words that resonate with its staff and honor its unique stories and history. That definition should be communicated consistently so everyone understands what giving is and what it does.

Giving Is Essential

The healthcare organization's ability to achieve its highest aspirations is directly related to the engagement and investment of the community. Everyone, regardless of job title, needs to understand that gifts are not "nice to have" but essential to have and should be able to articulate the role of and need for philanthropy. When grateful patients or members of the community express a desire to say thank-you or help, their interest never should be met with "thanks, but no thanks" or "the staff would love to have pizza." As stated earlier, everyone should be able to direct potential donors to the foundation and share the role giving plays in the organization's advancement.

Giving Is Noble

Philanthropy is a noble task. It is not about shaking a cup or twisting people's arms to persuade them to give. Some may consider asking for money an uncomfortable or undesirable obligation, so this work needs to be reframed as an opportunity and a responsibility to invite people to become a partner in important work that will have a positive impact on others and create a better organization.

Giving Puts Donors First

Philanthropy respects and honors the role of the donor. The use of funds, activities undertaken toward the completion of projects funded by giving, and the impact of those initiatives must be truthfully and consistently communicated to donors. This level of transparency breeds trust, an essential element of any genuine partnership. Anyone interacting with a donor should be forthright. Honest stewardship is effective stewardship.

Donors should be recognized appropriately for their gifts. Recognition should be dispensed in a fair and equitable manner and at a level consistent with good financial and organizational stewardship. Many organizations choose to formulate policies on recognition to ensure a "standard operating procedure" exists before a gift is made. One of the ramifications of such policy is that organizational insiders should not make commitments to name areas (e.g., a room or a unit) after people simply out of respect, as a sentimental gesture, or when, for example, someone retires. Those who "give away" a valuable naming opportunity break a social contract with donors who achieve such recognition only after giving at a significant level of investment.

Donors should know their gifts will make the greatest possible impact on the healthcare organization. They trust the healthcare organization to use gifts for their highest purpose and to manage charitable resources well. Philanthropy needs to be funneled through a united front—generally the foundation or development office—so that this covenant is kept. Rogue efforts to advance the interests of individual people or programs are not to be tolerated because they are not in the best interest of the organization or donors. All gifts—of any size and from any source—should go through a single, agreed-upon channel for consistent recording, recognition, stewardship, and management. Hospital staff should **never** initiate a solicitation without working hand-in-hand with the foundation. In healthcare organizations that do not enforce a strict standard of solicitation through coordination with the foundation, a single donor—particularly corporate donors—may receive requests from multiple hospital departments for money or in-kind gifts of their products. As a result, the hospital receives small, reactive gifts, and the donor is likely to think the organization is unclear about its priorities and has poor internal communication. Foundations have lost out on many major gifts because donors they had identified to participate in larger projects receive a request first from a rogue staff member. In such situations, the donor's goodwill is often directed to a lesser purpose, and while one department may benefit, the organization as a whole sustains a loss.

It is ethical to put donors first, too. The solicitor is responsible for ensuring the donor's best interest is safeguarded before the needs of the healthcare organization, and especially before the needs of the fundraiser, are met. It is always in an organization's best interest to place a donor's financial security, well-being, and values first, even if doing so delays a gift or causes the organization to lose out on the gift entirely.

Giving Is Partnership

Donors are more than dollars. They should be valued not only for their financial contributions but also for their advocacy in the community, connections to others who may care about the organization's work, and ideas for the organization's advancement. Donors who have made significant gifts to advance the organization's future should be invited to participate in ways beyond financial support. In short, donors need to be respected as vital partners; they are not substitutable means to an end. The organization must be willing to interact with donors meaningfully beyond the charitable exchange. For example, it might invite donors to join the design team for an area they wish to fund, include them in focus groups or meetings about the organization's future plans, or call them personally before significant news about the organization hits the front page of the newspaper. Inclusion of donors in activities and forums may test the mettle of organizations not accustomed to having "outside" people participate, but the long-term benefits of such inclusion outweigh any trials the organization may encounter as it acclimates to donor involvement on the inside.

Giving Is Personal

A culture of giving encourages all inside stakeholders, from staff to board members, to make an annual charitable gift commensurate with their means to secure and strengthen their shared future. However, compulsory giving by employees is strongly discouraged because it may breed resentment. While widespread support is a goal better fostered than prescribed at the employee level, it is a base expectation of executives and board members. This expectation should be clearly articulated at recruitment so they may make an informed decision to accept a leadership position in the organization.

CREATING CULTURE

Leaders may gauge their organization's stage of development toward a culture of philanthropy by reflecting on questions such as:

- Does everyone in the organization know what *giving* means?
- Do staff understand the rationale for philanthropy and the role it plays?
- Have people inside the organization seen the impact of giving firsthand?
- Do people know where to direct someone who wishes to give?
- Do employees engage others in philanthropy even if this responsibility is not included in their job description?
- Can everyone from frontline staff to board members explain how gifts are used?
- Is giving seen as an imposition or a noble way to engage others?

By determining their organization's stage of cultural development, leaders can define what still needs to be done to achieve a successful culture of philanthropy and have a starting point from which to work.

The CEO and other senior executives shape organizational culture daily whether they intend to or not. They are primary role models and expectation setters whose direction moves the organization to action. The behavior they exhibit and the values they espouse set the standard for normative behavior in the organization. Their verbal support and physical presence are essential to any culture-building effort. They must move philanthropy up the list of organizational priorities and set the expectation that philanthropy is an imperative endeavor in which everyone participates. This task is not easy. According to Edgar Schein (2010), professor in the Sloan School of Management at the Massachusetts Institute of Technology, culture is the most difficult organizational attribute to change.

Culture-Building Tools

- Presentations at employee meetings at all levels
- Standing agenda item or "mission minutes" in board meetings
- Signage throughout the facility about the opportunity to give
- Signage where people stop (e.g., elevators and bathroom stalls)
- Advertisements, news releases, and publications
- Employee newsletters, check stuffers, and time clock signs
- Physician newsletters and signage in parking garages and lounges
- Postings on the intranet and on screensavers
- Commercials on the in-house television channel
- Inclusion on internal evaluation scoreboards and in staff goals
- Inclusion in orientation for new hires and mandated annual staff training
- Annual employee giving campaigns or celebrations
- Talking points on the role of giving and on specific case statements to share in conversations with grateful patients and members of the community
- Inclusion in Twitter tweets and social networking site posts
- Inclusion in community benefit reports
- Mentions in op-eds or letters to the editor in local newspapers
- Donor recognition and project information displays in the facility
- QR (quick response) codes that can be updated with timely information
- Lanyards, badge pulls, or pins on clinical staff uniforms

The following steps are a structured, systematic approach to developing a culture of philanthropy:

1. **Evaluate** the existing organizational culture to see where positive strides have already been made and to identify large gaps between the desired state and the current environment. Important questions include:
   —Do staff know the organization has a charitable foundation?
   —Do they know what past giving has enabled?
   —Do they know the organization's current funding priorities?
   —Do they know where to refer someone who wants to help?
2. **Define** the attributes and characteristics that a successful culture of philanthropy would have in the organization. Ask thought leaders at all levels of the organization to define *culture* and *philanthropy*. From their input, create a definition of each that is accessible and understandable to all. For example, *philanthropy* is "sharing what you have to help and give hope to others." Also describe specific, observable indicators of a successful culture of philanthropy by answering such questions as:
   —What words would people use?
   —What behaviors would people exhibit?
   —How would people treat each other?
   —What roles would staff members play?
3. **Link** the desired behaviors and attitudes to the organization's mission and values to show how living the culture is an extension or a manifestation of the organization's vision and has a direct impact on patients and families:
   —Include philanthropy in the organization's strategic plan.
   —Ask everyone to commit to advancing this vision of excellence.
   —Have individual areas/service lines/leaders work with their teams to identify specific ways to demonstrate cultural values.

4. **Model** the behaviors desired at all levels so people can see these expectations in action. Have champions engender these behaviors in others. Leaders and board members influence staff, who in turn influence physicians, volunteers, and other allies.

5. **Communicate** that culture is integral to achieving the organization's highest aspirations. Decide how cultural behaviors, norms, and ideas will be translated to new employees. Use a range of communication channels, from employee newsletters to signage to the intranet to screensavers, even signs on the inner side of restroom stall doors, to reinforce the cultural message. Sustain and nurture the culture by implementing ongoing training, just as fire safety or Joint Commission requirements are repeatedly instilled.

6. **Embed** cultural expectations in job descriptions, individual performance goals, and institutional scorecards. Many top-performing organizations have found this step to be an interim effort until the culture has taken hold and philanthropy is "just part of what everyone does."

7. **Evaluate** outcomes to affirm that philanthropy has become a lasting cultural institution, not a flash-in-the-pan or flavor-of-the-month phenomenon. Culture is hard to measure, so define measurable outcomes that should naturally flow from the creation of a successful culture. Also define how people who are not exhibiting the expected behaviors and attitudes will be held accountable for their unwillingness to be part of the vision. While recruiting is difficult (especially for clinical positions), if a current staff member does not want to participate in the culture, it may be time for that person to seek another career opportunity.

8. **Celebrate** individual and collective successes to reinforce ideal behaviors and attitudes and to honor those driving the

culture. Celebrations can easily be infused in the organization as inspirational mission moments that celebrate employees and allies for upholding the culture and recognize donors for giving. For example, it can be powerful and affirming to invite a donor to an organizational forum to share why he or she chose to give. Also take time to celebrate

—allies who have taken significant action to educate, solicit, or steward potential donors;

—gifts to the organization that are particularly impactful or inspiring; and

—completion of projects funded in part or in whole by giving.

Recognition and celebration validate the organization's culture of philanthropy and the outcomes this culture enables.

Affirm the Healthcare Organization's Charitable Purpose

Nonprofit healthcare organizations need to act like charitable organizations. While healthcare organizations have budgets and streams of revenue that are disproportionate to the scale of many nonprofits, they are cautioned not to fall into the trap of behaving like big business. When healthcare organizations financially support and sponsor other nonprofit organizations as good corporate citizens and for marketing purposes, their participation needs to be strategic and appropriate. Many a donor has been dismayed after giving to a hospital and then seeing the hospital make a large gift elsewhere. Organizations are advised to thoughtfully articulate the reasons for their gifts to others and ensure recognition positions the organization as a partner, not a major benefactor.

IN SUMMARY

A culture of philanthropy that engages the entire organization and its allies establishes giving as a goal worthy of broad participation. It ensures the rationale for fund development is widely understood and shows that everyone has a role in advancing philanthropy regardless of title or position.

FOUR STEPS TO CREATING A PLATFORM FOR PERFORMANCE

1. **Communicate.** Educate employees and other key allies across the organization about philanthropy's vital role and about their opportunity and responsibility to be engaged in its advancement.
2. **Provide tools.** Give executives the information and training they need to be confident and successful. Ensure they are well versed in the rationale for philanthropy because they most often will be the ones to explain the role philanthropy plays in advancing solutions that will improve the health of the community. Also teach them the basics of solicitation and how to use storytelling to make the case for support.
3. **Give well.** Have executives and board members set an example through personal giving. Show employees why their gifts matter, and let them choose to step up rather than swallow the bitter pill of compulsory or pressured giving. Facilitate giving commensurate with financial ability by asking people to consider contributing the monetary equivalent of time increments rather than a set figure; for example, employees can donate 30 or 60 minutes of hourly pay per pay period. This system enables everyone to make a comparable commitment regardless of pay grade.
4. **Give wisely.** Create a policy about outbound giving. Gifts to other nonprofit organizations should be clearly aligned with

the healthcare organization's mission and values so donors see that the gifts are a natural extension of the organization's vision and community role rather than a confusing contradiction.

Interview with Doug Picha, President, Seattle Children's Hospital Foundation

Seattle Children's Hospital is the pediatric and adolescent referral center for Washington, Alaska, Montana, and Idaho. It is also the primary teaching, clinical, and research site for the Department of Pediatrics at the University of Washington School of Medicine. Seattle Children's has 250 beds and physicians in nearly 60 pediatric subspecialties.

QUESTION: Tell us about the rebranding of Seattle Children's. What were the primary objectives you wished to accomplish?

ANSWER: The primary objective was to evolve the brand to better represent what Seattle Children's had become and the aspirations for the future. For example, we had evolved to a top-five pediatric research organization and our foundation was a core asset to our brand, with advocates saying, "I think of Children's as a charity with a hospital attached." We wanted to elevate these two components to the same level as our hospital as the three pillars of our brand.

QUESTION: Has rebranding been a reflection of the organization's overall commitment to/culture of philanthropy?

ANSWER: Absolutely. Research confirmed the foundation was a vital part of who we are and what we wanted to become. This started with our CEO, Dr. Tom Hansen, who often states, "Philanthropy is everybody's business." I think

→

the results are evident in our fundraising efforts and the engagement of our staff and leadership. Here is a good example: A system-wide leadership conference retreat was initiated at Seattle Children's about the same time as the rebranding process was put in place. With our new brand as a backdrop [to the] conference, the CEO appropriately began the conference with a talk centering on how our strategic planning process was successfully helping us achieve our overall vision . . . Each of the presidents of the three entities (hospital, research institute, and foundation) followed him with our own state-of-the-state address. What this communicated to this audience of over 500 leaders in our organization was that philanthropy [is] an equally critical partner in the fulfillment of that strategic plan and vision. It sent a strong message and has made a deep impression.

QUESTION: What impact has the rebranding had on telling your story to the community?

ANSWER: It has provided a platform which now includes philanthropy in every message we convey. In short, it says, "The critical work of the hospital and research institute would not be possible without the generous support of the community (i.e., foundation)." It also reinforces a culture of philanthropy (i.e., private gift giving is critical to sustaining our mission).

QUESTION: If you had advice for healthcare CEOs on the integration of philanthropy into the overall brand, what would it be?

ANSWER: I think there is a long laundry list of ways CEOs can support the philanthropic activity within their organization, and branding is just one. My overall advice would be if you have a strong foundation or aspirations

$\longrightarrow$

to invest in this function, you should strongly consider integrating philanthropy. It is very important particularly now as private funding is becoming more important.

My further advice for CEOs and their relationship to their philanthropic enterprise would be to start with a commitment to either create or further enhance [their] culture of philanthropy with[in] their institution. It all starts there. If the sitting CEO is not committed to the current and long-term culture of philanthropy within their own shop, there is little hope philanthropy will be considered being incorporated into the brand.

There are many ways to measure a commitment to establish such a culture. Perhaps the two biggest commitments are to spend at least one-third of their time in the work of philanthropy and by their own personal philanthropic support. Both of these indicators are critical toward establishing a culture of philanthropy.

Incorporating philanthropy into the branding of the institution reinforces a message that their mission can only be accomplished and sustained with the continued generous support of the community.

QUESTION: What else do we need to know?

ANSWER: This project was successful because the foundation and marketing/communication department worked together from the start to develop strong synergy. For example, the foundation worked with marketing to incorporate the brand launch into the campaign celebration. But the real synergy comes from our structure: Marketing has two team members sitting in the foundation fully focused on marketing the foundation. This is key.

Why Everyone Needs to Be Engaged: A Story from Foundation Executive Carlton Long

Carlton Long (2011) is vice president of development and community services at East Tennessee Children's Hospital in Knoxville. This story recollects her experience at the former Mercy Health Partners (now the for-profit Tennova Healthcare), also in Knoxville.

"We received a very generous check in the mail from a donor I had never had contact with. The only thing that accompanied the check was a thank-you note from a lady who wanted to let me know how much she appreciated the kindness, compassion, and great care our hospital showed toward her adult nephew during the last week of his life. Her nephew had been initially treated for cancer at another institution but came to our hospital for his final days of care—therefore her reason [for] sending the generous check. Immediately I picked up the phone [and] called her to thank her and invite her to lunch. She then told me the story about her desire to send the hospital the $40,000 check.

Her nephew was not covered by any insurance. She was taking care of his bills and received the final bill from the hospital after his death. Noticing the hospital charges were in the $80,000 range and the reimbursement from Medicaid was only $1,500, she was shocked the hospital was not going to receive much for the excellent care they provided. The billing office at the hospital received a call from her stating she wanted to pay for her nephew's charges. On the other end, the billing clerk explained the hospital was not allowed to accept any more for the services, but

→

directed her that if she wanted to make a donation to the hospital foundation she could do that. The clerk explained the donation would then go toward helping others. Without the help of this billing clerk, this gift would have never been made to our foundation. Education on philanthropy and ways to give are necessary for all levels of employees. It starts on the front line."

CHAPTER 7

Aligning Project Selection

Billions are wasted on ineffective philanthropy.
Philanthropy is decades behind business in applying
rigorous thinking to the use of money.

—*Michael Porter, professor, Harvard Business School*

STRATEGY AND PHILANTHROPY are integrally connected disciplines when executed well. Effective fund development is rooted in the ability to enunciate a clear and compelling vision of what the organization could be if it achieved its potential. When strategy and philanthropy are disconnected, fund development becomes an arbitrary endeavor that is functionally indifferent to enabling high-value or low-value activities.

Alignment between the foundation's fundraising priorities and the healthcare organization's strategic plan is critical to optimize the opportunity philanthropy presents. The foundation exists solely to strengthen and sustain the healing mission of the organization. Therefore, the foundation's funding priorities are wholly dependent on its ability to frame and share the organization's vision for fulfilling its mission.

Donors want to be part of thoughtful and strategic efforts that advance the healthcare organization's highest ambitions, particularly when giving large amounts. Major gift donors are strongly inclined to direct gifts to benefit highly visible, high-priority, high-impact projects central to the organization's strategic plan and core mission. They are also more likely to restrict the use of their gifts to particular projects or service lines.

Donors give to big ideas. A vision that is incremental or uninspiring will not move them. Neither are they moved by organizational "needs." They are inspired by solutions the organization is uniquely qualified to implement. Thus, the organization needs to carefully select visionary projects that will enhance lives. In short, vision is the key ingredient of an urgent, compelling case for support that moves donors to action.

OVERCOMING INGRAINED OBSTACLES

Many healthcare organizations have difficulty integrating and aligning philanthropy and strategy. Some use philanthropy for initiatives that add value but are not essential. Others leave project creation and advancement to the foundation's discretion, and similarly, the resulting initiatives are tangential to the organization's core mission. Many organizations position philanthropy to take care of what is left after they have taken care of their priorities. None of these tactics leverages philanthropy because

- offloading low-priority projects to the foundation undervalues and poorly utilizes community giving, and
- donors do not want to fund remnants left on the chopping block after capital has been allocated to high-value projects.

A PROCESS FOR ENABLING ALIGNMENT

Strategic selection of projects for donor funding often depends on a clear and deliberate process that balances competing needs and values and transcends internal politics and power struggles.

Categorizing Priorities

It can be helpful to start the alignment process by dividing the organization's major projects into three separate "buckets":

- **Strategy projects** enable new capabilities, new services, expansion of services, research, and other significant enhancements of current offerings. These projects drive innovation and clinical leadership and have the potential to transform local healthcare. Such initiatives generally improve diagnosis and treatment or enhance the healing environment. Projects in this bucket are aimed at fulfilling the organization's highest aspirations.
- **Mission projects** provide clear community benefits but may not be supported by an existing or adequate stream of revenue. Examples include social work, child life services, health fairs, and prevention screenings. Medical services for those unable to pay are also included in this bucket; however, most donors are not interested in offsetting the financial burden of charity care and uncompensated care.
- **Maintenance/mandate projects** meet regulatory or other compulsory requirements. This bucket might also include building maintenance and equipment replacement.

Donors are drawn to projects that meaningfully advance the quality or availability of care, so the objective is to seek funding for initiatives from the strategy and mission buckets. Donors generally are not interested in projects from the maintenance/mandate bucket, even if those projects are crucial to daily operations. Philanthropy is about advancing solutions rather than fulfilling needs. However, by funding high-value projects that appeal to donors through philanthropy, the organization frees up capital for maintenance/mandate tasks. See the box titled "Funding to Enable Continuity" for information on seeking support for maintenance/mandate initiatives.

Funding to Enable Continuity

Donors are generally not interested in obligatory projects, such as the maintenance of power plants, elevators, parking garages, and fire safety systems or the replacement of aging or obsolete equipment, even if crucial to daily operations. Many donors feel that such projects are the basic responsibilities of running a business. However, in exceptional circumstances when an organization has no other means of funding such initiatives, asking for assistance may be a viable option. Organizations may gauge the appropriateness of requesting funding for continuity projects by asking the following questions:

- What is essential to provide an appropriate standard of care?
- What is critical to functional and safe operations?
- What is required by mandate or law for the organization to continue operating?
- Will help provide a solution that will enable the organization to return to sustainability, or is continuous crisis the organization's new reality?

Philanthropy positioned as a mode of survival is not sustainable, however. If donors receive consistent appeals to fund basic needs, their confidence in the organization will likely wane. Before going down this road, an organization should consider the effect such appeals might have on its credibility and on patients' confidence in its ability to provide quality care. Donors may give to an urgent plea once or even twice, but they do not wish to fill a widening gap of need.

Consider Donor Values

Once the organization has determined which of its high-priority projects are aligned with its strategy and mission, the next step is to identify which projects would likely appeal to donors. Donor-centric project selection matches initiatives with donors' values to motivate them to participate.

Donors generally seek projects that directly benefit people. Examples of projects that might appeal to donors include

- implementing technology that will enable new clinical capabilities and better outcomes;
- expanding building capacity or enhancing the hospital environment;
- launching clinical programs that add capability or anticipate emerging needs;
- enhancing social, emotional, and spiritual support of patients;
- improving community wellness through outreach and prevention initiatives;
- instituting innovation to improve quality or safety;
- advancing clinical research; and
- developing education to prepare high-caliber practitioners.

Ultimately, all these efforts directly enhance the physical, social, emotional, and spiritual well-being of patients, families, and other members of the community. The chief development officer's input is essential to evaluating the appeal of a project to donors and identifying known donors linked to similar projects.

Map It and Gap It

If several opportunities have strategic and donor appeal, a visual management system or gap analysis may help the organization refine its priorities. A simple priority map (Exhibit 7.1) can be created by placing projects along vertical and horizontal axes in order of increasing importance. The vertical axis represents the importance of projects from the organization's perspective, and the horizontal axis represents the appeal of projects to donors. The project placed in the top right box is the best match, reflecting both high donor appeal and high organizational priority.

A simple gap analysis (Exhibit 7.2) may also help the organization see where the proposed project stands and estimate the point to which additional investment could advance the organization toward the reality it desires to achieve. This type of analysis shows which project would have the most profound impact on patients and their families. While gap analysis can be subjective, it is a useful way of spurring discussion about organizational priorities.

Exhibit 7.1: Priority Map

Organizational importance	High system priority Low donor appeal Example: mandates	High system priority High donor appeal Example: technology
	Low system priority Low donor appeal Example: resurface parking lot	Low system priority High donor appeal Example: art

Donor interest

Exhibit 7.2: Gap Analysis

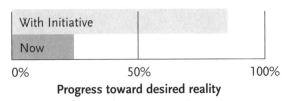

With Initiative	
Now	
0%	50%	100%

Progress toward desired reality

A Process for Achieving Alignment

- Select specific high-value, high-impact objectives from the strategic plan.
- Separate the objectives into strategy, mission, and maintenance/mandate buckets.
- Determine which objectives are associated with a service for which the healthcare organization is considered unique or superior in the market so the project eventually chosen will advance acknowledged excellence.
- Identify which objectives will add capabilities or enable better outcomes.
- Determine whether each objective is a business case, a mission case, or both; it is helpful to know which objectives can be initiated or sustained only with donor support.
- If the objective is technology, consider its useful lifetime. Items that have a short lifetime or are already moving toward obsolescence are not ideal projects for philanthropy.
- Prioritize the objectives in each bucket.
- Review top priorities for donor appeal. Would the project have a meaningful impact on a significant number of patients or on the community?
- Review projects for donor availability. Do enough donors have an interest in the project and the ability to give at the required levels?
- Identify projects that have committed or possible physician champions. Are there compelling and available advocates who could help engage donors?
- Determine the timeline for the initiative. Does the foundation have adequate time to identify and educate donors and secure their participation prior to project start?
- Submit a ranked list of the resulting top priorities to the foundation board for consideration.

The Lever of the White Coat

Once the organization has selected a slate of appropriate projects for philanthropy, a further consideration is the availability of a physician champion. As discussed in Chapter 4, the influence of physicians on prospective donors is too great to ignore. According to Bentz Whaley Flessner's (2010) 10th Annual Healthcare Survey, physicians have more influence on donors' gift decisions than do organizational leaders and board members. Further, a dedicated physician on the solicitation team can enunciate the clinical impact the proposed project will have. Therefore, in addition to considering organizational priority and donor appeal, the organization needs to choose projects that have a compelling and willing physician champion.

The Sensitivity of Timing

Another element of integrating philanthropy and strategic planning is identifying projects far enough out on the horizon to allow sufficient lead time to advance a variety of efforts, including

- finalizing a case statement articulating the vision;
- securing the internal support or votes needed to move the project forward;
- rallying champions and ambassadors who can help solicit;
- identifying, engaging, and soliciting prospective donors; and
- paying initial pledges to start cash flow to the project.

Ideally, the window between the selection/approval of the funding priority and the purchase/start of the funded project should be 18 months; for a large capital campaign, this window should be at least 36 months. Organizations also need to time public announcement of project plans congruously to ensure the message conveyed to all parties is consistent, accurate, and appropriate. Because top campaign gifts are customarily secured in advance of a public announcement to ensure project success, the timing of announcements should allow adequate time for this "silent" phase of a large capital campaign.

While the governing board of the healthcare organization retains ultimate discretion to approve a project or a program, waiting for governing board approval often limits or even closes the window the foundation needs to advance solicitation. On the other hand, the organization does not want to grant approval too early, especially when it is a public entity whose actions are covered by the local media; it does not want board approval to create an impression in the community that a project will go forward with or without donor support. People will not be motivated to give if they perceive their support is "nice to have" but not essential. Therefore, the approval process should be structured to enable key solicitation calls to be made privately to selected individuals before public announcement of the project.

For these same reasons, the campaign for gifts should end **on** or **before** the day ground is broken, equipment is acquired, or a program is started. The compelling, urgent case for support evaporates at that time. When a project proceeds and solicitation continues, the request for donor support looks more like a window dressing than an appeal critical to project advancement and places the organization's credibility in question.

Optimized Financial Goal Setting

Many institutions fall into the trap of setting goals for charitable investment by subtraction—that is, by asking the foundation to fund the gap the healthcare organization feels it is unable to fill— or by similar arbitrary methods. Monetary goals for philanthropy need to be closely tied to the capacity of the fund development organization, known or likely donors' interest in the specific project, the breadth of potential donors able to give at the level of financial investment required, and so forth. In other words, the goals need to be achievable and rooted in the reality of what the organization has raised in the past and is likely to raise in the current environment. In short, financial goal setting for philanthropy needs to follow a deliberate, information-driven process to position the campaign for success.

Audacious Leads to Excellent

Any hospital that sees unbounded organizational potential and dreams of making that vision a reality will be inspired by the story of Grady Memorial Hospital in Atlanta, Georgia. This public safety-net hospital has faced considerable financial challenges. Saddled with a self-pay patient load that often exceeds 50 percent of its total patients, it teetered on the brink of insolvency and even threatened closure. However, the hospital also had an inspired physician. Dr. Michael Frankel, chief of neurology, had a vision for a world-class program for stroke care at Grady. It was a plan he dusted off and presented to leadership on several occasions. Each time he was told his plan was not possible at Grady. In lieu of the big plan, incremental steps that could achieve parts of his vision were considered. But Frankel insisted that his proposal demanded excellence on a large scale, and ultimately his audacious dream won the day. When a visionary new CEO entered the picture along with a passionate board chair and an inspired donor who understood the transformative power of the opportunity, a $20 million gift enabled the creation of the Marcus Stroke and Neuroscience Center. This facility with leading-edge equipment and lovely aesthetics is a world-class oasis of excellence that raises the bar and the community's expectations for Grady. It also communicates to other facilities that "we can't do that here" is a limiting belief (Frankel 2011).

IN SUMMARY

Healthcare organizations that align charitable priorities with their strategic plan optimize the opportunity philanthropy presents. While this process requires diligence and coordination across the organization, integration and alignment will position charitable giving not just as a means of adding value but as a stream of revenue that enables the organization's highest aspirations. The best projects have strategic merit, donor appeal, physician support, an adequate time horizon for implementation, and realistic financial goals.

SEVEN STEPS TO CREATING A PLATFORM FOR PERFORMANCE

1. **Make a list.** Create a list of emerging investment opportunities that both reflect the organization's highest priorities and are likely to appeal to donors.
2. **Create a process.** Implement an ongoing, structured process for identifying the best projects and presenting them to the foundation or development office for their consideration. Enable broad ownership of objectives by involving the executive, operations, finance, and philanthropy teams in the process and asking them to validate the plans.
3. **Make it official.** Include explicit expectations for philanthropy in the organization's strategic and financial plans.
4. **Set appropriate goals.** Make sure monetary goals for philanthropy are realistic by assessing the capacity of the development organization, the availability of motivated and capable donors, and the support of champions and allies.
5. **Cross-pollinate.** Invite foundation board members to the organization's strategic planning retreat, and invite the organization's board members to the foundation's philanthropy retreat. Keep everyone on the same page to align the case made to the community.

6. **Designate a seat.** Add the development officer to the strategic planning committee and other executive forums to integrate philanthropy and other areas of the organization.

7. **Remember what donors want.** Donors are interested in strategically aligned projects championed by organizations that exhibit financial stability and sustainability. They do not fund bailouts or backfill budgets. Donors respond to successful organizations that have big ideas.

Interview with William S. Littlejohn, CEO and Senior Vice President, Sharp HealthCare Foundation/Sharp HealthCare, San Diego, California

Sharp HealthCare touches about 800,000 people each year. Sharp serves San Diego County's 3 million residents and includes four acute care hospitals, three specialty hospitals, and two affiliated medical groups. Sharp HealthCare operates 1,900 beds, has 2,600 physicians and 14,800 employees on staff, and is supported by three nonprofit philanthropic foundations.

QUESTION: Why is alignment between strategy and charitable priorities important?

ANSWER: With Sharp's five-year strategic plan as our guide, the foundations of Sharp HealthCare are aligned with the greater goals of the organization, ensuring philanthropic support is effective and impactful and allowing us to pursue the margin of excellence we believe our patients and their loved ones deserve.

Our fundraising priorities align with the greater goals of the organization:

- *Caring:* Provide clinical and community programs and services, reflecting our commitment to continually strive

→

---

for a level of care that sets community standards and exceeds expectations.

- *Learning:* Fund research and education, allowing Sharp to conduct actionable research that allows us to significantly improve quality of care.
- *Building:* Support construction of new medical facilities, ensuring San Diegans, today and in the future, receive care in state-of-the-art facilities.
- *Growing:* Expand knowledge and competency of physicians and staff.
- *Leading:* Advance technology to save lives and improve quality of life.

QUESTION: What specific steps have you taken to achieve alignment at Sharp?

ANSWER: Philanthropy is a key component of Sharp HealthCare's strategic planning process. Each year, a five-year financial projection is performed. The resulting five-year plan provides the financial direction for the organization and serves as a feasibility analysis by quantifying the financial impact of Sharp's strategic initiatives. The philanthropic component of Sharp HealthCare's five-year operating cash and capital plan is a nationally recognized best practice; the Sharp foundations have provided more than $100 million *in cash* to the five-year plan in the eight years [that] ended September 30, 2010. Combined, the foundations fund 10–15 percent of Sharp's capital expenditures annually. Over the next five years, the Sharp foundations are projected to provide more than $80 million; such donations support the continuation of patient care programs throughout the system, as well as directly fund capital acquisitions necessary for both ongoing operations as well as strategic

→

investments. The five-year plan demonstrates the strong link between financial and philanthropic success and the ability to fund capital improvements. The plan is contingent upon strong operations, implementation of strategic initiatives, and fundraising, all of which are necessary to support Sharp's planned capital investments. The plan is relied upon by Sharp's outside rating agencies, Moody's Investors Service and Standard & Poor's, in their evaluation of Sharp's financial strength and growth over each five-year horizon.

QUESTION: What benefits have you seen as a result of alignment?

ANSWER: The foundations of Sharp HealthCare are dedicated to raising $100 million to support a $700 million plan to provide advancements at Sharp's respected regional medical centers and specialty hospitals, from infrastructure and research to state-of-the-art technologies and the best possible patient care.

QUESTION: What advice would you give to a healthcare CEO considering tighter alignment of strategy and charitable priorities?

ANSWER: The new model for healthcare is one of *philanthropy*, marked by the elements of best practice, including strategic alignment with the institution, creating a strong and visible institutional culture of philanthropy, and focus on acquisition and cultivation of donors toward long-term and beneficial relationships. This new model, however, requires rigor, discipline, and high expectations of performance.

Interview with Roger E. Seaver, president and CEO,
Henry Mayo Newhall Memorial Hospital

Henry Mayo is a 227-bed, not-for-profit community hospital
and trauma center with more than 400 physicians and 1,300
employees. Henry Mayo is the only hospital in the Santa
Clarita Valley in California.

QUESTION: What was the "call to action" that led you
to ensure tight alignment between strategy and your
community case for charitable support?

ANSWER: The call to action for the tight strategic
alignment [of] the hospital and the community came
during my first month as CEO of this community
hospital. The history of the hospital post the Northridge
earthquake of 1994 produced a unique financial crisis that
threatened continued viability as a community hospital.
The hospital had financed required seismic upgrades
with short-term bank loans and the use of all financial
reserves. Operational performance prohibited capital
investments within a two- to three-year forecast. However,
the community, a generous benefactor, and the medical
community supported the need for an expanded service.
Only through philanthropy was this possible in the desired
time frame. The creation of a state-of-the-art breast
center was accomplished in 15 months. This significant
example provided clarity [that] our hospital [can] respond
to community need [and] a charitable desire to support
and [has] the ability to say "Yes, let's do it!" Our future
integration of strategic priorities and philanthropic
support was born.

→

QUESTION: What specific steps have you taken to ensure alignment between hospital strategy and foundation funding priorities?

ANSWER: The specific steps to ensure strategic alignment [are] the integration of fund development executives with the senior leadership of the hospital in all planning processes as well as clarifying community need. One of the strategic imperatives in our planning process is to evaluate all funding sources, which include operating performance, issuance of long-term debt, and philanthropy. Our strategic plan requires a balanced-portfolio approach to resourcing our capital and operating needs. Further, our action plans and tactics require the hospital support of charitable opportunities, the support of philanthropic activities, donor identification strategies, and stewardship of the funded programs/projects for the benefit of our community.

QUESTION: How has alignment enabled philanthropy to make a more leveraged impact at Henry Mayo?

ANSWER: Alignment has helped lead us to balance our total resources to consistently finance new programs, provide enhancements, and fund strategic priorities with a recognition that the positive role of philanthropy will be maximized as we successfully deliver true benefit to our community. This alignment is building the necessary consistent infrastructure that completes the dream with reality and then focuses our stewardship to consistently convey the benefits of philanthropy to those who receive the benefits. Alignment has also enhanced trust for willing donors, as they recognize our commitment to request funds needed for important projects and their ability to see their gifts in use.

→

QUESTION: What advice would you give to a healthcare CEO who wishes to more tightly align hospital strategy and philanthropy?

ANSWER: My advice to any healthcare CEO [who] wants to strategically link the hospital strategy with philanthropy is that you approach it in a businesslike manner. Integrate the strategic planning process, adopt best practices in philanthropy, and expect the businesslike approach to be measured on results with a focus on long-term benefits. I would caution against looking at philanthropy as short-term solutions to long-term benefits. Equally important to the strategic planning process is the need for the hospital to understand [its] role in stewardship, donor identification, and service excellence for all future benefactors.

QUESTION: What else do we need to know?

ANSWER: I think the untold story for nonprofit hospital CEOs includes the tremendous value we can provide to those able and willing to support our philanthropic needs. One of my biggest thrills in integrating philanthropy with the mission of the hospital is to experience the absolute joy of a donor who has the ability to make a significant difference, and we were thoughtful enough to ask them for their help. If you have not experienced this, it is one of those truly enjoyable aspects of facing the challenges of healthcare delivery in the nonprofit hospital sector. Get on board! You are missing a great part of our professional fulfillment.

CHAPTER 8

Supporting Vibrant Giving Through Excellent Service

Unless you have 100% customer satisfaction . . . you must improve.

—Horst Schulz, former chief executive officer,
The Ritz-Carlton

SERVICE EXCELLENCE AND positive care experiences inspire confidence and loyalty that can translate to powerful giving. Evidence shows that grateful patients and families are key to building a major gifts pipeline. In one study, 50 percent of affluent individuals said a recent personal or family experience would strongly motivate them to make a charitable gift to a hospital (Bentz Whaley Flessner 2010). In another study, 88 percent of healthcare organizations' top donors had a previous personal or family care experience (Advisory Board Company 2007).

Patients and families present a significant opportunity for finding and engaging the best prospects for charitable giving. The revolving door of the healthcare organization continuously refreshes the list of individuals who are grateful for the care they or a loved one received. The healthcare organization's aim is to create an optimized care experience that inspires a desire to give.

THE IMPORTANCE OF SERVICE

The concept of *service* has received a lot of attention in recent years. Efforts to enhance the patient service experience became more focused after the Centers for Medicare & Medicaid Services publicly released data from the Hospital Consumer Assessment of Healthcare Providers and Systems (HCAHPS) survey, the first standardized national survey of patients' perspectives of hospital care. The release of these data made the patient experience more transparent to the general public and enabled consumers to make informed decisions when selecting a healthcare facility.

The HCAHPS survey focuses on aspects of the patient experience that motivate consumers to choose a healthcare facility, such as communication with caregivers, cleanliness, and pain management. For foundations and their clinical counterparts to leverage the opportunity the patient experience presents, leaders need to understand which of these elements shape the inclination to give.

Success at securing grateful patients as donors is highly correlated with patients' and families' perceptions of the **quality** of the care experience. Because most patients do not have the knowledge or experience required to evaluate **clinical** quality, most patients evaluate what they understand: quality of **service**. An evaluation of service is also a reflection of confidence: If caregivers fail to perform simple tasks, such as responding to call lights in a timely and attentive manner, how can patients trust them with formulating plans to save lives?

Donors seek organizations that deliver on their promises. Caregivers' inability to execute basic tasks raises questions about the organization's ability to deliver on a big dream.

SERVICE LEVERS THAT DRIVE GIVING

A survey of healthcare decision makers (i.e., those who choose care for themselves and for others, such as children and elderly parents) in the United States sheds light on which perceptions of the patient experience are connected to the conversion of a grateful patient to a donor. The survey found that approximately one in five consumers polled (20.5 percent) had made a charitable gift to their hospital (Binder, Deao, and Taylor 2011). Donors were more likely than non-donors to (Binder, Deao, and Taylor 2011)

- rate the overall quality of care as excellent,
- say the hospital exceeded their expectations,
- say their loyalty was attributable to their interactions with hospital staff, and
- have a close friend or relative who received inpatient or emergency care.

While it is almost impossible to identify specific triggers that ensure a grateful patient becomes a donor, it is possible to identify beliefs commonly held by patients who became donors. Of patients who believe their hospital (1) provides excellent quality care and (2) always exceeds their expectations, about one-third (30.4 percent) have made a charitable gift to the institution (Binder, Deao, and Taylor 2011). Patients' likelihood to give increases dramatically with the addition of a third element: excellent hospital employees. When consumers said they found **excellent quality care** that **exceeded expectations** and **excellent employees**, the percentage of donors more than doubled, from 20.5 percent to 48.4 percent (Binder, Deao, Taylor 2011). While many hospitals focus their service metrics exclusively on providing excellent quality care and exceeding expectations, hospitals may want to expand their emphasis to include perceptions of frontline staff to foster a service environment that inspires someone to give.

Every Interaction Matters

The perception that staff are excellent develops as a result of many interactions. A patient may consider a wide range of indicators, including, for example

- perceived clinical competence;
- emotional and social support;
- treatment of patients as individuals, not as "names on charts";
- positive and professional interactions between team members;

- expressions of genuine concern;
- demonstrations of respect;
- attention to details; and
- tone of voice.

When patients and families come to a hospital, their service experience is shaped by everyone they encounter: the volunteer giving directions at the front desk, the registration clerk, the phlebotomist, nurses, physicians, the discharge manager, the parking garage attendant, the billing clerk, and many others. Each person has an opportunity to create an impression about the organization's commitment to quality and service and to demonstrate her attention and compassion. Thus, every person in the healthcare environment shapes an impression that will lead to the willingness to make a gift—or not.

A single oversight is all it takes for a patient to change his perception of his visit: one rude interaction, one slip of attentiveness, or one poorly chosen word. Once a patient feels a service failure has occurred, even the most gracious foundation staff member cannot undo the bad impression.

While needs and desires are as individual as patients, employees in the healthcare organization can take a proactive and systematic stance to anticipate and fulfill patient expectations.

FOUNDATIONS AS EXTENDERS OF SERVICE

Many foundations take a hands-on approach to service and use the few precious days a patient is in the organization for care to express gratitude for giving or to build a warm relationship. Visitation or concierge programs facilitate connections with current donors or patients who have financial ability. Solicitation **never** occurs during these visits. The visitor greets the patient, asks if her experience is going well, coordinates service recovery if it is not, and offers appropriate services, such as bringing the patient a pillow, sending a fax, or providing a newspaper—simple courtesies that enhance the patient's physical comfort or provide social/emotional support. Full-fledged concierge programs are more robust and may have one or more staff members dedicated to 24/7 service.

Many foundations screen patient names to focus visitation programs' activity by sending patient information to an outside service that uses data or modeling to assign scores for financial ability and charitable inclination. On the basis of this information, the foundation prioritizes visits to those with the greatest capacity and likelihood to give. These data screening relationships are underscored by business partnership agreements and other controls to ensure compliance with Health Insurance Portability and Accountability Act (HIPAA) privacy guidelines.

Many hospitals that do not engage directly with patients during a care experience say their reluctance is rooted in fear of violating HIPAA. However, visitation programs and grateful patient engagement programs are consistent with the guidance of a variety of reputable resources on appropriate practice under HIPAA, including the Association for Healthcare Philanthropy (www.ahp .org/Resource/advocacy/us/HIPAA/Analysis) and the American Hospital Association (www.aha.org/aha/content/2002/pdf/HIPAA

Points to Consider When Building an In-Facility Visitation Program

- *Timing*: Determine meaningful connection points during the patient experience (arrival, admission, inpatient stay, discharge, post-discharge).
- *Focus*: Decide who will be the focus of your efforts. (Donors giving at certain levels? Patients identified by research? Others?) How will you handle those who ask to maintain their privacy by being excluded from the hospital directory?
- *Clearance*: Ensure plans are compliant with HIPAA, state law, and hospital policy. Ask yourself: "What is the minimum amount of patient information I need to do my job well?" Do not obtain all the information you are permitted to collect on someone just for the sake of collecting information. Allow people as much privacy as possible.
- *Information*: Create plans and systems to manage data appropriately. Seek automated integration of the information management systems supporting the prospect screening programs. Maintain call reports from visits and other connections made.
- *Training*: Address the rules of engagement for personal interactions with patients. Train staff on appropriate interactions with patients in the clinical environment and educate them on clinical and safety signage (e.g., NPO ["nothing by mouth"], droplet precautions).
- *Culture*: Include the entire organization in the effort (e.g., nursing, housekeeping, dieticians, volunteers). Train everyone on how to refer grateful patients who express gratitude.

$\longrightarrow$

- *Execution*: Plan how the program will work (e.g., staffing, processes, resources).
- *Follow-up*: Develop plans for converting gratitude to giving (e.g., caregiver recognition programs, direct mail, follow-up calls, tours).

FundraisingAdvisory.pdf). Simply, HIPAA defines healthcare foundations as part of hospital operations. As such, hospital foundations are permitted to access a range of demographic data, such as name, gender, date of service, address, phone number, and e-mail address. Foundations are prohibited from accessing data that disclose the patient's reason for medical treatment. Many foundations collaborate with healthcare organization privacy and compliance leaders to establish protocols for appropriate practice.

The purpose of visitation and concierge programs is not to create a two-tiered care system; all patients receive the same quality medical care that donors and prospects receive. Foundation staff should never intervene in the provision of care. The function of visitation is simply to provide hospitality and customer service to enhance patients' experience. In hospitals where it is not legally permitted or organizationally accepted for the foundation to have direct interaction with patients (e.g., in Canada and in some states), it will be more important for clinical leaders to fulfill this role to ensure a positive patient experience.

For visitation programs to be effective and appropriate, a range of other questions need to be considered to respect the individual's needs and right to privacy and to fulfill the organization's responsibilities:

- **Would a visit be well received?** Respect for patient privacy and patient wishes must be paramount. Patients who do not wish to have visitors generally have their name removed from the public directory or have a code in their medical record. If

A Practical Guide for Patient Visits

- Wear your name badge.
- Check in with the nurse manager upon arrival whenever possible. If he is not available, introduce yourself to appropriate clinical staff on the floor before visiting the patient so they are aware of who you are and what you are doing.
- Look for signals outside the patient's room that a visit might not be appropriate. Notice call lights or signs warning of various precautions, asking visitors to see a nurse before entering, or specifying no visitors.
- Knock before entering the patient's room, and ask if it is okay to enter. For the duration of the patient's stay, this room is her home, so treat it as such.
- Be brief. Plan for your visit to last no more than five minutes. Visits may run more than five minutes, however, if you are invited by the patient or his family to stay longer.
- Acknowledge the patient by name when possible when you enter the room. Use formal titles unless you genuinely know the person (e.g., "Good morning, Mr. Smith!").
- Introduce yourself to the patient and any family or visitors in the room. Identify yourself as a representative of the foundation.
- Out of respect for the patient and in compliance with HIPAA, never ask the patient directly or indirectly about her medical condition. Keep questions generic; for example, instead of asking "How are **you feeling** today?" you might ask "How are **things going** today?"
- Focus on the patient, not on others who may be more alert or responsive. Do not talk about the patient as if he

→

were not present. Let the patient do most of the talking if possible.

- Respect the patient's personal space. Never touch the patient unless she invites contact by reaching out to shake your hand or making a similar gesture. Sit down only at the invitation of the patient. Never sit on the patient's bed. Leave the room during medical treatments or discussions between clinical staff and the patient.
- Affirm the patient's care team. Call the nurse or physician by name (if you know it) as you assure the patient he is in good hands.
- Never give what could be construed as medical advice. Do not speculate about a patient's condition, orders, procedures, or discharge date.
- Ask if there is anything you can do to make the patient's stay or environment more comfortable. Offer personal service and assistance as appropriate.
- Thank the patient for her charitable support if appropriate.
- If a patient expresses a concern, communicate the issue to the nurse or to the appropriate hospital department so it can be resolved through the proper channels. Close the loop by letting the patient know to whom you have communicated his concern.
- Before leaving the room, ask if there is anything else you may do to be of service.

Thanks to Kelly DeGregorio of Martin Memorial Foundation and Greg Pope and Amy Snodgrass of Saint Thomas Foundation, whose best practices were considered in creating this guide.

a patient has requested anonymity or privacy, the foundation should decide if any interaction should occur. For example, it might be appropriate to leave a note or a card for the patient at the nursing station, letting her know that the foundation understands she requested privacy but that foundation staff are available if she needs assistance.

- **Is it a good time?** Staff need to ensure visits are not an imposition and do not place patients in an embarrassing situation. The patient might be in a physical location (e.g., the intensive care unit) or have clinical accoutrements (e.g., an oxygen mask) that could make a visit socially uncomfortable. It is also important to note if there are social/ emotional issues that would make the moment a wrong time to visit; for example, the patient might be nearing death or privately visiting with a pastor. Finally, visits should be made at times that do not interrupt care delivery. Early afternoon usually is a good time to visit because many tests are performed in the morning and physicians often make their rounds before midmorning and in the late afternoon.

In visits to non-donors (people who have not given before but who may or may not have been asked to give), a primary intention is to facilitate a future relationship with the patient. Therefore, staff should try to "keep the door open" after the patient is discharged from the hospital. For example, one might offer to

- call the patient when he arrives home to see how he is doing,
- take the patient on a behind-the-scenes tour of the facility,
- include the patient in future invitations to events of interest,
- visit with the patient when he arrives home,
- meet over a cup of coffee when the patient feels better, or
- follow up with the patient regarding his interest/issue.

Development professionals need to think more broadly about who their prospective donors may be, both for visitation and eventual solicitation: Data show that the close friends or family members of patients are just as likely as patients to become donors (Binder, Deao, and Taylor 2011). These visitors are keenly aware of hospital staff's actions and the service they provide (or lack thereof). In some cases, they are more aware than the patient of the service provided by staff. By seeking to better understand the expectations of both patients and their guests, hospitals will not only provide better care and increase word-of-mouth referrals but also cultivate more donors.

CAPTURING THE OPPORTUNITY THAT SERVICE PRESENTS

Focused efforts to engage grateful patients as donors have not been the ambition or the reality in many healthcare organizations. A 2011 survey of affluent donors found that two-thirds had not been

---

Education Opportunities During the Patient Experience

- Posters in elevators, patient areas, and waiting rooms
- Skins on the outside of elevator doors
- Printing on folders containing discharge information
- Information in the patient directory (i.e., the hospital phone book placed in patients' rooms)
- In-house television channel
- Printing on patient meal tray liners
- Guest Internet home page
- Giving walls or plaques honoring previous donors
- Information displays and brochure holders
- Signs near cash registers in food service areas
- Tent cards on tables in food service areas
- Messaging on staff badges

---

asked by the hospital, by any method, to make a gift (Bentz Whaley Flessner 2011). Development officers admit current acquisition strategies are not ideal; two-thirds of development professionals say they "do not do a good job" approaching past patients, and one in five hospital foundations said they make "no effort at all" to contact patients (Grizzard and Association for Healthcare Philanthropy 2007). However, studies consistently show opportunities to ask grateful patients to give. At least 20 percent of respondents to surveys in 2008, 2009, and 2010 indicated a "grateful patient" program would motivate them to give to their hospital (Bentz Whaley Flessner 2009, 2010, 2011).

Comprehensive grateful patient programs consider natural points of engagement of guests in the facility:

- Arrival at the facility: What signage or displays support philanthropy?
- Registration: Do staff know and acknowledge donors?
- Outpatient point of service: Are there ways to express gratitude?
- Inpatient room arrival: What in the room supports philanthropy?
- Inpatient stay: Are donors acknowledged and new relationships fostered?
- Meal delivery: Is there an opportunity for messaging on trays?
- Television: Can the hospital's in-house channel include information on giving in its programming?
- Discharge: What do patients receive when leaving?
- Post-discharge follow-up: How does the foundation reconnect after the care experience?

After the care experience, foundations have a variety of tools at their disposal for follow-up with grateful patients. Traditionally, hospital foundations have reached out to former patients through broad-based donor acquisition programs, such as direct mail or telephone solicitation, that touch a large number of people at a low cost. While such programs have created workable donor pipelines, savvy organizations also use a combination of wealth and psychographic screening to identify individuals who are most likely to have the interest, value alignment, and financial ability to become major donors, and they include those individuals in a personalized follow-up program that may include follow-up letters, "qualification" visits to determine interest, invitations to behind-the-scenes tours, and other efforts usually reserved for the organization's best prospects. While this type of program demands additional resources from the organization in terms of staff time and dollars, it is more likely than traditional methods to engage donors who could be inclined to make a major gift.

IN SUMMARY

An excellent service experience yields a number of benefits. It helps patients heal, affirms patients' decisions to choose a particular organization for their care, inspires donors to share their positive story with others who might at some point require care, and cultivates a fulfilling work environment. It not only attracts new donors but also gives them confidence that the organization delivers on its promises. Yet few hospitals act systematically to understand and to address what patients value in the nonclinical aspects of their care experience. Progressive foundations and health systems that embrace the three key triggers of donor support—having **excellent employees**, providing **excellent quality**, and always **exceeding expectations**—have the capacity to literally double the number of grateful patients who make a charitable investment.

THREE STEPS TO CREATING A PLATFORM FOR PERFORMANCE

1. **Create a place at the table.** Include the chief development officer or another key foundation representative on the

healthcare organization's service excellence team. This person's role is to ensure philanthropy is represented and to facilitate collaboration between hospital and foundation efforts to enhance the clinical service experience.

2. **Seek high-value interactions.** Provide clinical and executive leaders with a list of major donors and high-potential prospects who are currently inpatients to visit on their rounds. The goal is to ensure they are having an excellent service experience, thank major donors for their past involvement, and simply demonstrate concern and respect.

3. **Focus on engaging grateful patients.** Invite grateful patients to be part of the healthcare mission. Think about opportunities during the patient experience to educate and engage them, and follow up with them once they are home to ask them to make a charitable gift. Place special emphasis on those most capable of helping the organization. Grateful patient engagement programs can be developed at a level of sophistication and intensity that works with your budget and staffing resources.

CHAPTER 9

Making a Compelling Case for Support Through Storytelling

The case for support "should aim high, provide perspective, arouse a sense of history and continuity, convey a feeling of importance, relevance and urgency, and have whatever stuff is needed to warm the heart and stir the mind."

—Harold J. (Si) Seymour,
noted trailblazer in the practice of development

MANY PEOPLE GIVE to healthcare organizations because they want to be part of a group that is touching and changing people's lives. An organization's case for support demonstrates its important, compelling vision and the validity and urgency of its plea for community support. The case interprets and breathes life into the organization's mission in an honest, meaningful, and inspirational way. It galvanizes donors to choose the organization's cause over the many other causes worthy of their support.

The case is more than a collection of facts. It is a living, emotion-infused document that validates the human impact of your proposed plans. It presents visionary solutions to important problems, not the organization's needs or wants, and shows why your organization is uniquely positioned to advance those solutions. It also builds internal consensus and ownership and raises community awareness of both the organization and the cause. This document is usually the first to introduce the organization's project to the community and is a talking piece for gauging community support and concerns. On the basis of community feedback, it is edited and then repurposed for a variety of donor communications, from collateral materials to solicitation letters.

Exploring how an organization successfully makes a case for giving, Adrian Sargeant, fundraising scholar, and Jen Shang, philanthropic psychologist, note: "Three basic types of evidence can be used to make a convincing case to donors. You can appeal to their emotions, making them believe passionately that supporting your organization is the right thing to do. You can appeal to their reason, convincing them intellectually that supporting your organization is the logical thing to do. Or, you can appeal to the credibility of your organization, showing donors that your organization has the ability to keep its promises and complete the work it sets out to do" (Sargeant and Shang 2010).

The most compelling cases for support deftly weave a communication that mixes all three: emotion, reason, and credibility. Simply, the case for support melds an inspirational story and an informational investment prospectus in one seamless communication. A

The Case for Support

The case for support answers a variety of questions for prospective donors, such as:

- What is the problem for which a solution is proposed?
- What solution does the organization wish to advance?
- What are the implications of the problem and the solution?
- How is the organization uniquely qualified to propose and execute the solution?
- What mission does the organization exist to fulfill?
- How can community support be an enabler?
- How can donors get involved, and why should they?

---

well-written, substantive case statement enables donors to decide whether the project reflects their values, aspirations, and good judgment. An emotional story opens people's hearts to the organization and inspires feelings of connection. Logic and facts support the case that the organization is uniquely capable to execute the proposed plan. The element of credibility shows the organization is a well-managed, consistent steward that merits their confidence and trust.

In making their case for support, healthcare organizations have an obligation to ensure the community understands how they are paid and why they need philanthropy. In Bentz Whaley Flessner's 2010 study "What the Affluent Think of Giving to Healthcare," respondents' most common objection to supporting hospitals charitably was "I pay for my healthcare through health insurance" (44 percent), followed by "other organizations need my money more" (33 percent) and "hospitals are a business and do not need my gift" (24 percent). Forty-two percent of affluent responders said they might be motivated to give if hospitals helped them "understand why [their] support is needed."

Excellent resources are available on what a case for support should include, what questions it should answer, and how to craft it. Many organizations do an excellent job of cataloging the merits that give them credibility or the logical validity of the case, but they often fall short on the third leg of the stool: instilling genuine emotion. This important, elusive element is the focus of this chapter.

THE ART AND SCIENCE OF STORYTELLING

Storytelling is a powerful way to engage others in the organization's healing mission. Whether in written narrative form or told face-to-face in conversation, stories tap into the basic human inclination to connect. Stories are an ideal medium for showing the mission in action. Mission storytelling is also a high-impact but easy way to get executives, board members, physicians, and other advocates actively engaged in advancing the cause of philanthropy.

The field of psychology called *behavioral economics* shows that giving is fundamentally an emotional rather than a rational process. Multiple studies indicate that the majority of major gift donors have had a personal or family care experience with a healthcare organization. Nonetheless, the foundation needs to create rich, sensory

---

Considerations for Crafting a Great Case for Support

1. Know what you want to accomplish when sharing your case for support. Are you testing community interest? Increasing understanding? Driving action?

2. Show why you are uniquely qualified to advance the proposed solution.

3. Know your target audience. What are the values/worldview/demographics of the prospective donors you wish to reach?

4. Use a voice and style consistent with the organization's brand and image.

5. Develop a compelling message to share your audacious goal and the impact it will have on people.

6. Integrate storytelling to create an authentic, emotional thread that connects people to your mission.

7. Make the case personal. Show prospective donors what is in it for them, their community, and so forth.

8. Make your call to action specific and understandable so donors know how to respond.

9. Anticipate questions and objections so you can address them proactively.

10. Present your story in a visually appealing, accessible format (use white space/bullets/headlines) that enhances the sensory experience (use photos, video, or QR codes) but is not so "produced" that donors feel you have been a poor steward of resources.

---

surrogate experiences through which people can encounter the mission vicariously.

Since the days of Aesop, stories have been used to teach lessons, pass down history, and share human experience. Stories ingrain the hopes and values that shape our lives, transfer fundamental elements of culture from generation to generation, and illuminate connections between people. Stories can be effective whether they are as structured as a Shakespearean play or as simple as a slice of life shared with a neighbor over a backyard fence. Powerful stories inspire others to retell them, are memorable, and have a fundamental authenticity. Just as people are drawn to books and movies that evoke certain emotions, well-crafted mission stories emotionally engage people in the organization's work and bind them to the institution.

A variety of truisms apply to mission stories, each of which is discussed in the sections that follow.

Truism One: Emotion Trumps Reason

Emotional intensity connects people to the organization's healing work. When people see someone going through emotional upheaval in a film, for example, nerve cells in the brain called "mirror neurons" fire, and viewers feel what the person on the screen feels.

According to behavioral economists, people do not behave rationally; rather, people behave irrationally in predictable ways. In other words, the emotional, intuitive right brain makes decisions, and then the analytical, logical left brain collects evidence to support those decisions. For this reason, the emotional connection must be made first; people need to be moved to want to find out more about the organization.

A paper from the Graduate School of Education at Harvard University shares more on this subject (Ritchhart 2000):

> Our emotions have projective power over our thoughts. They act
> as filters to form our desires, furnish our capacities, and to a large

extent rule our immediate thoughts. As we encounter fresh situations, become faced with novel problems, or grapple with new ideas; our emotional response to each of these sets in motion the initial allocation of our mental resources. In essence, our first "read" of a new situation is always centered in our emotions, feelings, and attitudes. . . . When we feel empathy for another's plight, our emotion may help us to direct our energies to doing something about the situation. . . . Our emotions act as magnets to either pull us into action or channel our energies in a particular direction.

Another behavioral study further demonstrates this point: A fundraising appeal was made to study participants by the relief organization Save the Children. Some were given a picture and told the story of a starving seven-year-old girl named Rokia. Another group was given information about Rokia along with statistical information about 17 million starving people in the same region in which Rokia lived. All study participants then were asked to consider giving money to relieve starvation in Africa (Small, Loewenstein, and Slovic 2004). Those who saw the photo and heard just the story of Rokia gave 66 percent more than those who were given both information about Rokia and the famine data. The participants who gave the most were given the least information; in other words, the story of one suffering child moved participants much more profoundly than did the rational case for giving.

Princeton psychology professor Danny Oppenheimer sums up this phenomenon in one sentence: "People give less when they are thinking analytically" (Kadet 2010). Therefore, if statistics inspire less empathy and willingness to give, healthcare organizations should be selective about the facts they include in their appeals rather than cram their proposals full of statistics. It is best to stick to facts that elucidate the case or lend credibility to the organization's ability to advance the solution.

Most important are the "wow" stories that happen in the organization every day. Frontline staff and physicians are rich sources of stories about people whose lives were saved or transformed or could have been if the proposed project had already been in place. By creating a repository of mission stories to share with staff and the community, the organization builds philanthropic culture, understanding, and interest.

The caveat is to know where to draw the line. Emotion should not be evoked to the point of causing distress in the potential donor. Sargeant and Shang (2010, 69) note that while fear, pity, and guilt have all been shown to increase the number and size of gifts, efforts to produce these emotions must be handled carefully: "Their use should be strong enough to demand action, but not so strong that they become personally distressing to the donor. At this point, stimulating emotion becomes counterproductive and donors deal with their distress not by giving but by avoiding the communication."

Truism Two: The Power of One

In the last decade, more than 500,000 people died in the Darfur region of the Sudan in Africa as a result of mass genocide. Bodies were piled up on the side of the road and discarded in shallow ditches. Babies and children wasted away from malnutrition after their parents were killed. It was a scene of immense horror and death. However, when people went out on the world stage and asked others to help the condition of these suffering people, few responded—but not because they did not know the conditions were atrocious or that the issue was important. It was simply because people could not emotionally connect with or even conceive of the idea of 500,000 dead.

Nicholas D. Kristof (2007) of the *New York Times* wrote an editorial about the phenomenon called "Save the Darfur Puppy." In the piece, he talks about a series of studies by psychologists who were trying to understand why "good, conscientious people" were not moved by the genocide. He remarks, "Time and again, we've seen that the human conscience just isn't pricked by mass suffering, while an individual child (or puppy) in distress causes our hearts to flutter." He says activists often share the dramatic scale of mass human tragedy—likely in hope of shocking people into action—not understanding that "the more victims, the less compassion" (Kristof 2007). This "psychic numbing" limits the human capacity to feel.

An article in *Wired Science* about a study of jury verdicts for people charged with exposing others to toxic substances reinforces this phenomenon and gives it a name: the "scope-severity paradox." The study found that the greater the number of victims, the less harsh the sentence was for the crime. Psychologist Paul Slovic of the University of Oregon explains, "[The research] shows that as the number of people who are victims of some problem [increases]— whether it's a crime or a famine—the responsiveness to it, and the likelihood of taking action to reduce the problem, decreases." He continues, "It has to do with the way empathy works. People empathize with people by putting themselves in the other person's shoes. The more shoes there are, the harder it is to empathize with any single individual. People don't multiply their feelings of empathy by the number of people involved" (McNally 2010).

Other research also validates that people are more likely to respond to individuals than to groups. However, it suggests that humans are "perfectly capable of responding emotionally to groups" but "steel themselves against it" to protect the psyche (Cameron and Payne 2011). Social psychologist Elizabeth Dunn of the University of British Columbia says, "[I]f you really took everything to heart, to the full magnitude that all these disasters really deserve, you'd probably be sitting at home rocking yourself in a closet all day" (Cameron and Payne 2011).

Whatever the rationale for why people respond this way, the implications are clear: Stories need to revolve around a single individual whom donors can relate to and connect with on a basic human level. Much like a parable shares a universal lesson through a simple story, healthcare organizations can use stories to illustrate the broader impact of a philanthropic project by sharing the experience of an individual who could benefit from the initiative. While a story about the impact of a medical program may include detailed or complex information, people can process and understand that information much more easily if it is presented in the context of one person's journey. The single journey is analogous to the potential impact of the program on a community.

Truism Three: Strong Stories Need Strong Characters

Vladimir Propp (1928), in his *Morphology of the Folktale*, identified archetypal characters that drive the action of any story, factual or fictional. Each character plays a role in advancing the plot. The following three roles are most prominent in healthcare stories:

- *Hero/victim:* The story revolves around this figure. The hero generally is not the organization but an appealing person who has been put in a difficult situation involuntarily. In the healthcare setting, this person typically is a patient but could be a researcher seeking new treatments or a physician seeking to enhance or expand care.
- *Villain/obstacle:* The villain represents the struggle or conflict that attempts to thwart the hero's aspirations. The villain does not have to be a person. In healthcare, illness or injury usually plays this role.
- *Prize/desire:* The prize or desire is something the hero hopes to gain or strives not to lose. In many fairytales, the desire is the princess, who stands for the ultimate objective of the hero's quest. In healthcare, the prize typically is a return to health or a cure.

Complex healthcare stories may also include the following characters:

- *Helper:* The helper enables the hero to achieve the desire. In healthcare, this role is ideal for a physician who becomes a champion to the patient. Alternatively, the helper could be the healthcare organization or a program, treatment, or technology.

- *Donor/provider:* Fittingly, another character in Propp's typology is the donor/provider. The donor is an intercessor who prepares the hero for the challenge ahead or provides a "magical agent." In healthcare, those who make charitable gifts certainly infuse a dose of magic in the medicine by enabling progress and advancing care.

When at least the three elements of hero, villain, and desire are brought together, a compelling story is created. For example, Dorothy would just be a child from Kansas if *The Wizard of Oz* did not involve a witch who blocked her aspiration to reach the Emerald City, and *Star Wars'* Luke Skywalker would merit little interest without Darth Vader trying to foil his plot to quash the evil of the Galactic Empire. The interplay of the elements creates the tension and interest that engage the audience/listener.

Of the elements of a good story, the most important is the hero/victim. This character needs to garner empathy and be relatable. The audience needs to feel that the hero/victim is innocent—that is, he did not create the situation at hand. An obvious but extreme example of an unsympathetic hero/victim is a patient who sustained life-threatening injuries as a result of a car accident he caused by driving under the influence of alcohol. Donors respond most to stories about someone they feel is suffering from consequences beyond his control. If donors feel the hero in the story could be responsible for his condition, they are less likely to give, and thus the number and amount of gifts decrease (Piliavin, Piliavin, and Rodin 1975).

Villains can also be hard to portray—especially when they are nameless/faceless diseases, such as cancer or heart disease, rather than a well-defined person people can mentally picture. The key is to attribute sufficient characteristics to the villain so donors understand and picture it as something they want to rise up against and fight.

Truism Four: Every Story Needs a Plot

Like all good stories, mission stories need a plot that will engage and carry people through the information that explains the impact of the healthcare organization's work.

Dr. Bruce Fraser (2010), a researcher on the Faculty of Classics at the University of Cambridge, observed that theories of narrative point to consistent storylines—possibly more stereotypical than archetypal—from which all stories flow. In her book *Beyond Buzz: The Next Generation of Word-of-Mouth Marketing*, Lois Kelly (2007) shares nine storylines people like to discuss. All of these "buzz-worthy" story types stem from a basic conflict between elements of the story or from a conflict with people's preconceived notions of the world.

One storyline is particularly suited to shaping healthcare stories: David versus Goliath. In the biblical story, a young man, dressed in just a tunic and armed with a simple slingshot and stones, fights a sword-wielding giant dressed in armor and wins despite the tremendous odds. The "good fight" of the underdog against seemingly unconquerable giants, which in healthcare take the forms of cancer, heart disease, extreme prematurity, and so forth, rouses people's emotions. Stories of patients who fought the odds of recovering from their disease or fought their way back to health from injury make people want to aid them in their struggle.

Other appealing healthcare storylines involve the following themes:

- *Human hope:* The authentic hopes and values of an individual resonate with people's own beliefs because these elements are part of basic humanness. This storyline may be particularly appealing to organizations that have religious or ethical underpinnings that connect people to a presence greater than themselves. Authenticity cannot be stressed enough. To be effective, stories must be revealing, personal, and intimate; they must disclose dreams and fears.

- *Discovery:* Stories of medical miracles or emerging innovation that flies in the face of human expectations and conventional wisdom challenge people to look at the world differently.

Truism Five: Substance Beats Flash

Love Endures Even Cancer, a beautiful video produced by the *New York Times* (Jones 2011), tells the story of a young man named Gavin Snow, who finds out he has stage three melanoma just months before meeting his girlfriend, Haley Tanner. The setting for the video is immensely simple: The couple sits in plain chairs in front of a white background. The production is also simple: Their story is told entirely in their own words and is interspersed with still photographs of their life together. However, this understated video packs a powerful punch. It deftly shares raw, genuine emotion and pulls viewers through the experience of a vibrant young man fighting cancer and facing a tragic, early death. This moving piece is an excellent example of a story that grabs people's attention and has substance that supersedes the need for fancy, expensive production.

While many marketing departments crave or even insist on highly produced collateral materials and videos, the power of the message is far more important than the finesse of the design. The following guidelines are recommended for production of a clean, professional presentation at minimal expense:

- Stories presented on paper should be accessible to the reader and visually appealing. Headlines, bullet points, and sidebars enable readers to skim the document easily and glean key points. Many effective proposals have been rendered on a simple color printer.
- Powerful stories can be captured on video with an inexpensive handheld camera and edited with desktop software. The trick is to have patients speak for themselves and to use simple film or still photos relevant to what the patient is saying to add visual interest.

Truism Six: Focus on the Benefits

Many stories, especially those about an innovative piece of new healthcare technology, tend to relate features in numbers and technical terms. Consider this excerpt from an article on the Diagnostic Imaging website (Freiherr 2008):

> The compact, 128-slice [CT] scanner can be sited in a room measuring 365 square feet and can be scaled to deliver 256 slices per rotation if the needs of the facility grow . . . The new system has the same gantry rotation, 0.27 seconds, as the . . . 256-slice scanner and delivers the same 120 kW power. Its . . . x-ray tube technology enhances spatial resolution.

While the features of this technology may be interesting to a narrow audience, this description would leave most laypeople with more questions than answers and would not convey the benefit of having one of these scanners. A donor reading a case statement about the acquisition of this piece of equipment would want to know how this technology would improve care.

Consider a pair of sunglasses with the following features:

- Color: black
- Material: plastic
- Type: unisex

While those features contribute to the appeal of the sunglasses, people care more about the benefits they derive from the sunglasses—for example:

- They protect eyes from UV rays.
- They reduce glare.
- They look stylish.
- The wearer is more likely to slip by the paparazzi unnoticed.

Therefore, while donors may not care that a CT scanner has 128 slices or a 0.27-second gantry rotation, they will care that the scanner will be taking more images that will enable physicians to make more accurate diagnoses, which in turn will enable someone to heal faster. They may also care that the CT scanner has a faster scan time so a patient does not have to stay still as long and the experience is more comfortable. They are also likely to care that it would limit patients' exposure to radiation and thus make scans safer.

Truism Seven: Happy Endings Are Not Required

Healthcare marketing tends to tell stories of terrible situations in which the hospital swooped in and provided care that enabled everyone to live happily ever after. Most stories in real life do not resolve so neatly, and the ones that do turn out perfectly leave nothing for a donor to help.

Unfinished or unresolved stories show donors their help is needed and give them an opportunity to step forward and take meaningful action to close the story. Consider the story of a woman who was diagnosed with cancer. She possibly started with surgery and then went through rounds of chemotherapy and maybe even radiation. She fought for a long time to get to the point where the doctor told her the tests show no further evidence of disease, and she felt she had won a huge victory. However, before she walked out the door, the doctor told her she has to return in six months for another scan to ensure she is still free of cancer. Even if that scan turns out clear, at some point in the future she likely will have to return a second time for another scan. Thus, her story did not end. Her fight is not over. She is better for now, but the threat is not entirely resolved. Unfinished stories such as this one identify the point of wellness to which the patient has traveled and suggest that someone will need to intercede to keep the patient well.

Truism Eight: Be Relatable

A wonderful video called *Historia de un Letrero* (translated: *The Story of a Sign*) by producer Alonso Alvarez Barreda, originally entered in the 2008 Cannes Film Festival online short film competition, tells the story of a man asking people for financial help. He is sitting on a sidewalk in a park, with a sign propped up next to him that reads, "Have compassion. I am blind." People walk by and look at the man, and some throw coins into the can in front of him. One coin, thrown carelessly, misses the mark and hits the sidewalk. Nobody is moved by the man's plight to do more for him.

Soon, a man walks by, sees the blind man's sign, and stops. He takes the sign, flips it over, and writes on the back. He replaces the sign and leaves. After the sign is changed, many, many more people stop and put money in the can to the point that it is flowing over. At the end of the day, the man who changed the sign walks by again. The blind man asks him what he did to the sign, and the man replies that he "wrote the same, but in other words." The new sign says, "It's a beautiful day, and I cannot see it."

The lesson is simple: To touch others, the message must be relatable. Most people have never been blind and cannot easily put themselves in the blind man's shoes. However, they have experienced the beauty of a sunny day and are saddened at the thought of never seeing one again. In that context, everyone understands the blind man's plight.

Truism Nine: Be Specific

The book *The Dragonfly Effect* by Jennifer Aaker and Andy Smith (2010) tells the story of two young men, Samir and Vinay, both diagnosed with leukemia. Because of their Indian descent, there are few probable donor matches for them in the bone marrow registry. Their friends mount a campaign via social media to tell the story of Samir and Vinay and their loving families in hopes of making people realize that these relatable young men have lives and experiences not so different from their own. In just 11 weeks, the campaign secures 24,000 bone marrow donors.

A pivotal element of the campaign's success was its specific, understandable call to action: Register as a potential bone marrow donor to help find a match and save the lives of the two men. It is not enough to say "please help" or "we do great work you would want to be part of and hope you will do what you can." People need to be given a clear, concrete way to exercise their desire to help.

Secrets to Great Stories

- **Share the impact your case for support would have on an individual.** A personal story is a powerful way to connect emotionally with potential donors.
- **Be resonant.** Tell stories that connect with people's values.
- **Use emotion, but do not resort to drivel or shock factor.** Stories should be neither sappy nor so upsetting that donors shut them out. Share stories that are powerful but not over-the-top.
- **Be authentic.** Be authentic, genuine, and honest when telling stories. Feature identifiable people in the community as characters.
- **Be relevant.** Make the story relevant to the donor. Show him why he should care and what is in it for him and the community.
- **Make it concrete and easy to process.** Help people readily understand what you are telling them and what you are requesting.
- **Tell it well.** Great stories move on the power of strong verbs and words that paint pictures.
- **Be specific.** Give people a concrete, understandable way to help.
- **Do it right.** Ensure compliance with HIPAA when sharing patient stories.

Truism Ten: Create a Consistent Brand Experience

In his monograph *Good to Great and the Social Sectors,* Jim Collins (2005, 25) notes that brand is a significant lever to convincing supporters to "believe not only in your mission, but in your capacity to deliver on that mission." Storytelling is part of building an experience of your hospital's brand. As Patrick Hanlon (2006) shared in his book *Primal Branding: Creating Zealots for Your Company, Your Brand, Your Future,* "When you are able to create brands that people believe in, you also create groups of people who feel that they belong. This sense of community is at the center of psychologist Abraham Maslow's famous hierarchy of human needs. . . . It is an essential human truth that we all want to belong to something larger than ourselves."

In crafting the case and stories that make up an organization's brand experience, hospital foundations must understand the value and appeal of their brands and know who their "brand lovers" are. It is also important to create a consistent donor experience of the organization in terms of messaging, voice, and style across all communication channels. Direct mail, websites, fliers, brochures, thank-you letters, videos, and other collateral all explain the organization's rationale for fundraising the same way so donors know what to expect from the relationship. Consistency also builds trust. Inside and outside the organization, the same numbers need to be used to explain hospital revenues, the value of the proposed project for the community, and so forth.

Be Yourself

As ambassadors for the healthcare mission, staff have an opportunity to share genuine passion. Most people do not take up a profession in healthcare lightly; they work in the field because they care about the plight of other human beings, are interested in the way medicine can transform lives, or were inspired to do so for some other meaningful reason. Healthcare has also personally touched many of these people, whether through a family member's experience or through their own. When they share their stories, they have unsurpassed credibility as professionals who do what they do not just because they are paid to do it but because of their beliefs and values.

Final Thoughts

The following points offer additional advice to those crafting mission stories:

- **Be authentic.** Be genuine, credible, and honest when telling a story. Feature real people who are identifiable in your community. Most people who have been through a significant healthcare episode are happy to tell their stories because they achieved a victory and are proud to say the healthcare organization enabled them to overcome their situation and thrive.
- **Tell your story in plain language**. Skip the healthcare jargon. For example, do not talk about *oncology*; talk about *cancer*. Do not say *cardiac*; say *heart*. Use words that are accessible to the general population. Even acronyms taken for granted, such as NICU, need to be translated to "neonatal intensive care unit" and then explained as the unit that cares for the sickest, most vulnerable infants.
- **Do not be too politically correct.** *Poor* paints a much clearer picture than does the term *economically disadvantaged*. People do not connect emotionally to the word *disadvantaged*, but images immediately come to mind when they hear the word *poor*.
- **Walk the fine line between problem and dream.** In many healthcare organizations, a gap exists between current capabilities and what they dream of being. Be careful not to denigrate what the organization has or erode confidence

in the current level of care it provides. Instead, point out opportunities to achieve a higher standard.

- **Paint a picture.** Details are what make a story sensory enough to remember. Create a palpable "word picture" that sticks in people's minds. How did the details look, sound, and smell?
- **Do not stop with a first draft.** The best writing is the rewrite. Put the story aside, let it sit for a while, and then go back and edit it.

IN SUMMARY

Great case statements and mission stories are memorable communications that people connect with emotionally and easily recount to others. Meaningful stories evoke values, such as love of family, and wrap an urgent vision and a call to action into a compelling narrative. Done well, they are a powerful tool for engaging others in the organization's mission.

THREE STEPS TO CREATING A PLATFORM FOR PERFORMANCE

1. **Find "wow" stories in your organization.** Share the impact your case for support could have on an individual. People are more likely to connect emotionally with an individual's plight than with a group's.
2. **Train your storytellers.** Teach development staff, executive team members, board members, and other staff members how to tell stories well so you can deploy an army of advocates.
3. **Set up procedures for clearance.** Always ensure compliance with HIPAA when using patients' stories. Put plans and processes in place to secure permission and releases.

CHAPTER 10

Gaining Insights About Donors

When we put our hope in devices and skills
without appropriate focus on donors,
we rarely succeed.

—*Joshua M. Birkholz, principal,*
Bentz Whaley Flessner

PHILANTHROPY IS DRIVEN by genuine relationships with
people who have the vision, interest, financial capacity, and motivation to become donors. How does a foundation find these people? It is valuable to know who the most likely donors are and
what is most likely to inspire them to be part of the organization's mission.

Each year more than 80 percent of gifts to charitable endeavors come from individuals (Giving USA Foundation 2011). Of
these gifts, more than 90 percent come from living people; the
rest are bequests left by people who have passed away (see Exhibit
10.1). While the remaining gifts are attributed to foundations and
corporations (approximately 20 percent), more gifts effectively
from individuals are "hidden" within these sources because in
private grant-making foundations and privately held businesses,
the family or owner generally makes decisions as an individual
and then deploys the funds from another financial resource he or
she controls.

Exhibit 10.1: US Giving by Source (in billions)

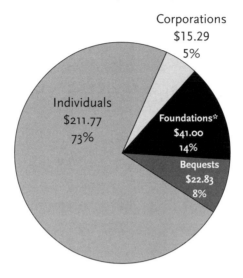

Corporations
$15.29
5%

Individuals
$211.77
73%

Foundations*
$41.00
14%

Bequests
$22.83
8%

Source: Giving USA Foundation (2011). Used with permission.

THE "TYPICAL" DONOR

Foundations need to know the characteristics of "typical" donors to be able to engage and communicate effectively with them. While donor types vary from organization to organization, the following generalizations may guide foundations to people who are likely to have a charitable interest in the organization's mission.

Demographic information about past donors to charitable organizations, including healthcare organizations, is a starting point:

- **Age:** Charitable giving typically increases with age, peaking between ages 50 and 64 (Independent Sector 2002), while healthcare donors tend to be slightly older, primarily between ages 50 and 70 (Russ Reid 2010). Many healthcare donors are empty nesters who have reached peak earning years but are not yet worried about outliving their financial resources.

- **Income:** Giving understandably increases with household income. However, studies show giving is a U-shaped phenomenon: Households having the lowest and the highest incomes give the largest percentage of their annual income. This distribution is due in part to the number of retired donors who have reduced annual income but have accumulated assets over their lifetime (Sargeant and Shang 2010).
- **Education:** The amount and frequency of charitable gifts made correlate with donors' education level.
- **Home ownership:** Homeowners give more often.
- **Marital status:** Marrieds tend to give both more often and in greater amounts than singles do.
- **Children:** People who have children give more often.

Who Needs to Be Engaged?

- Who is **passionately devoted** to your cause?
- Who has **used the services** provided by your organization?
- Who are the **champions** sharing and explaining your vision?
- Who are the most **philanthropic**?
- Who are **influential thought leaders** people listen to?
- Who are **well-networked connectors** who can open doors?
- Who has the **financial capacity** to meaningfully participate?

Once you have answered these questions, ask:

- What **relationships** do you have with these people?
- Are their **values aligned** with your mission?
- What **financial resources** do they have to contribute?

And finally, ask:

- How many of these people are currently engaged by the organization?
- What is your plan for engaging those who are not yet involved?

A point on which data diverge is whether the healthcare donor is more likely to be a man or a woman. A study of affluent households with an income of $200,000+ found that women (53 percent) were more likely to support healthcare than were men (47 percent) in general, but men (45 percent) were almost twice as likely as women (24 percent) to support community hospitals (Bentz Whaley Flessner 2010). Another study of donors at all income levels also found that women were more likely to give: 57 percent of women gave to healthcare causes, while 49 percent of men did (Russ Reid 2010). Anecdotally, women are considered more likely to give to healthcare because they typically are the primary healthcare decision makers in families; women encourage their spouse to seek medical care and choose when and where to take herself and her children for care.

WHY DONORS GIVE

Donors choose to give to healthcare organizations for a variety of reasons, all of which are extensions of donors' personal value system. While most donors' motivations are mission-centered and outwardly focused, some donors give for less noble reasons, including

- **guilt** (driven by a desire to compensate for shortcomings by doing good),
- **social aspiration** (prompted by a wish to be associated with an "in" crowd), and
- **validation** (spurred by a need for public recognition and personal affirmation).

Mission-centered donors' motivations include

- **social obligation** (urged to "give back" because they are in a fortunate personal situation),
- **tradition** (inspired to give because their family has always done so), and

- **personal experience** (moved to contribute following a significant episode of care).

Most donors are drawn to healthcare because of this third point: Their lives have been personally touched. An overwhelming 88 percent of top donors to healthcare state that they or a family member received care at the recipient facility (Advisory Board Company 2007; see Exhibit 10.2). These donors' gifts are rooted in values such as

- **civic commitment** (to acknowledge the importance of healthcare for the community),
- **gratitude** (to express appreciation for care received),
- **compassion or sympathy for others**, and
- **remembrance** of a loved one (to pay tribute).

See Chapter 8 for more detail on what motivates grateful patients and their families to give.

Exhibit 10.2: Percentage of Top Donors with Previous Personal/Family Care Experience

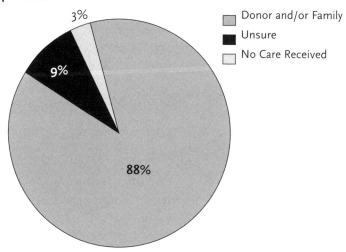

---

1. Philanthropy is a noble endeavor rather than an outstretched hand.
2. Donors are essential to success and merit treatment as such.
3. Donors give to enable the good they have in mind, not to meet the organization's needs.
4. Donors' financial security and well-being must be safeguarded, even when doing so conflicts with securing a gift.
5. The organization has relationships with donors. They are not just names on spreadsheets.
6. Solicitation is not the end of a process; it is the beginning of a partnership.
7. Sharing the impact of a donor's gift provides the donor an emotional return.
8. Doing the right thing is always better than doing the technically correct thing.
9. The Girl Scout song has an apt message for philanthropy: "Make new friends, but keep the old; one is silver but the other gold." Keeping friends beats having to find new ones.

AFFIRMING THE FUNDAMENTALS

The likelihood that a person will give to a healthcare organization also depends on whether fundamentals of the donor relationship are in place. While these truisms have been described under a variety of names, they can be remembered and summarized as the principles of connection, alignment, resources, and execution (CARE):

- **Connection:** Relationships are rooted in valuable connections between prospective donors and the key allies and staff of the healthcare organization. It is almost impossible to move from fundraising (characterized by low-value, transactional giving) to philanthropy (characterized by more significant giving enabled by partnership) without a credible and influential relationship between an ambassador for the healthcare organization and a donor.

- **Alignment:** Alignment of values and interests is critical to donor engagement. Alignment is the sum of many elements, including a warm regard for the institution and a belief that the organization provides a community benefit consistent with the donor's values and priorities. People have a choice of many charitable organizations through which to express their virtuous intentions, and they select one organization over the others because of this alignment.

- **Resources:** To give at the major gift level, donors must have sufficient financial resources, including disposable current income or assets accumulated over a lifetime. While people of any financial capacity can be valuable friends, those who take on key roles in transforming the organization must have the financial capacity to do so.

- **Execution:** A charitable mission to provide a broad community benefit is not enough. The development organization must take a systematic approach to identifying, educating, and engaging prospective donors in advancing the organization through philanthropy.

FOCUSING EFFORTS

Many development organizations build relationships incrementally over time by identifying prospective donors, engaging them in base-level donor acquisition and renewal programs, and growing the relationship through major and planned gift programs (see Exhibit 10.3). High-performing development organizations use strategic tools beyond general demographic research and the CARE fundamentals to optimize prospect selection. Electronic

Exhibit 10.3: Donor Pipeline

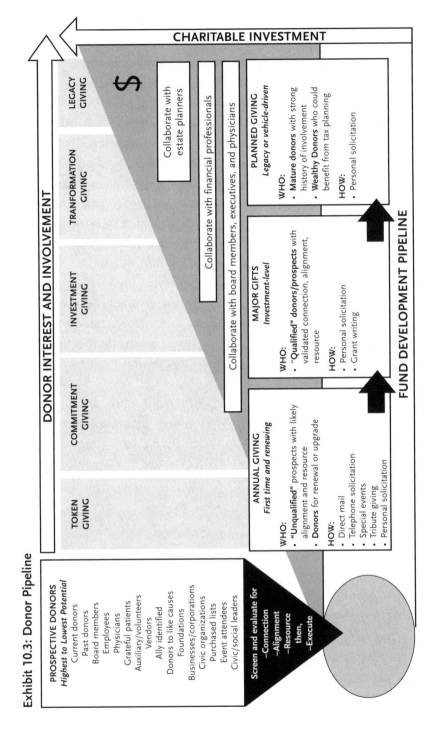

screening can help the foundation focus its efforts and set priorities for staff time and financial resources by identifying indicators such as financial capacity, value alignment, and past charitable giving to other causes.

While healthcare leaders and boards might be uncomfortable using electronic screening tools out of fear of violating people's privacy, these tools are no different from those that marketers use when mailing credit card offers and catalogs. The key is discrete storage and use of personal information. The data are never to be used for voyeurism; their purpose is to enable strategic management of prospects. As one author poignantly said, "Without a system to identify those constituents most likely to become valid prospects, the development staff might as well affix a list of constituents to a bulletin board and throw darts to determine which ones are to be the subject of their efforts" (Nicoson 2010, 55).

Assessment Through Financial Screening

Wealth screening services benchmark prospective donors' financial capability to give. Most services use publicly available data to determine prospects' assets, such as real estate holdings, investment portfolios, and other significant resources, and assign an estimated annual household income and giving capacity to each individual. While prospective donors using sophisticated financial management strategies can hide assets from screeners, foundations still often derive a good indication of their financial capacity from the quantity and quality of the assets that can be identified. Other services use modeling to assign financial capacity. Both methods sometimes underestimate capability but rarely overestimate it, so they offer valuable baseline information.

Financial capacity alone, however, does not make someone a good prospect. Many organizations fall into the trap of adding people to their prospect lists simply because those people have money. Wealthy people may or may not care about the organization's

Ensuring Sound Ethics in Screening

Prospect research is a well-established and common professional practice used to identify and engage the most promising potential donors. Research often includes collecting demographic information, financial information, lifestyle information, and information on past charitable participation. The data used for analysis are almost always publicly available. However, research needs to be thoughtfully and sensitively undertaken to ensure it is a tool for enhancing engagement rather than an exercise that donors might see as an invasion of privacy. While most fund development professionals already adhere to codes of professional ethics that stress privacy, confidentiality, and respect, here are a few practical thoughts on structuring a program to ensure donor confidence and comfort:

- Do not collect data for the sake of collecting data. Use research to seek actionable, meaningful information that helps establish someone's connection to the organization, value alignment for the cause, or financial resources.
- Do not store or retain data that could be sensitive or embarrassing to donors. If you would not want them to see it in their record, you should not be keeping it.
- Do not store health information you are not supposed to have, such as medical diagnosis, unless that information is self-disclosed by the prospective donor or otherwise appropriately obtained.

When used effectively and appropriately, prospect research helps fund development organizations prioritize their resource allocations and make more appropriate engagement plans for donors. Instead of relying on hope and intuition, it embraces the benefits of a world in which information is readily accessible.

mission. For an extreme example, an organization might see the immense financial capacity and deep commitment to philanthropy that American talk-show host and media mogul Oprah Winfrey has and consider her a potential prospect. However, unless she has a direct connection to the organization, she is not a valid prospect. The CARE fundamentals must be in place for a donor relationship to work.

Identification of prospective donors tends to stump many healthcare organizations, particularly those in smaller towns and rural areas, because they see conspicuous consumption lifestyles as indicative of wealth and do not see a lot of people exercising these behaviors in the community. However, flashy lifestyles are not a reliable indicator of who does or does not have the ability and inclination to give. In *The Millionaire Next Door*, Thomas Stanley and William Danko (1996) debunked the idea of what millionaires look like, saying most

- live well below their means,
- own non-current-model cars,
- live in modest homes in middle-class neighborhoods, and
- do not own status symbol luxury goods and material possessions.

Countless examples bear these data out; many people with wealth accumulated it by living conservatively. This actuality is another reason to use screening services to identify prospects who have more financial resources and giving capacity than one might anticipate.

Understanding Through Psychographics

Marketing tools use psychographic information to uncover the values, lifestyles, and personal preferences of people who have given to the organization in the past, both to identify others who would have the propensity to become donors and to target communications. While the psychology that influences donors' motivations is interesting and helpful, it is not intended to be used to manipulate prospects. The information simply helps organizations better understand and respond to donors' needs and create a fulfilling donor experience. Philanthropy is always about genuine relationships.

Identifying Known Donors

Screening can also mine databases of known donors to other charitable organizations. Such databases contain publicly available financial data and other information, such as donor recognition lists and newspaper coverage of gifts.

Using Screening Data Well

Consider a healthcare organization that wants to send a direct-mail piece aimed at acquiring new donors to everyone who had been a patient over the last year—for example, 100,000 people. Of those patients, 70,000 had commercial insurance or Medicare, so they make the first cut as likely having some financial ability to give. By screening the HIPAA-allowable demographic data on these 70,000 people, the foundation narrows this population to 25,000 people who have demonstrated financial capacity and have responded to direct-mail offers in the past. By running these 25,000 people through psychographic screening, the foundation can tailor its messaging to each household depending on identified interests— for example, some households might be more likely to respond to a message emphasizing "driving excellence," whereas others might be more inclined to react to a message emphasizing "helping the less fortunate." In short, an organization can narrow 70,000 pieces of homogenous mail to 25,000 pieces of resonant mail that are more likely to attract new donors.

Key Questions to Ask Donors to Uncover Purpose and Value

Age   **Questions of Significance**

50–60 • What are your core family values? What is important?
- Who are your role models?
- Who/what inspires you?
- When did you know you should be in the career you chose?
- What messages do you communicate to the people who work/train with you?
- How do you reward yourself?
- What wakes you up in the middle of the night?
- What are you grateful for?
- What are your life's goals?
- How should you help your children pursue their passions?
- If you had died last week, what would happen to your family?
- What are your family's assets?
- What has been your most meaningful experience in philanthropy?

60–70 • How does your family make important decisions?
- What is the meaning of your life?
- What does "service beyond self" mean to you?
- In business, how did you define success?
- Who were your mentors?
- How can one make a difference in the community/world?
- How much is enough to leave to family?
- How much is too much? (entitlement syndrome)

→

- How would you honor others through philanthropy?
- How can philanthropy perpetuate your values?
- Besides _____, what other organizations do you support? Why?
- How do you know when your gifts are making a difference?

70–80
- What has been important in your life?
- What values are so important as to compel you to promote them?
- When people speak your name years from now, what would you like them to say?
- Whom did you mentor?
- What are your family's shared dreams?
- What are you striving for?
- What's your proudest moment/greatest regret?
- If it is no longer money, what is it that motivates you?
- How can one fulfill the dreams of others?
- What will give you peace at the end of your life?
- What is your monument to the world?

80+
- Is there anything more you would like to accomplish?
- Would you do it all over again?
- How does money bring meaning in your life?
- What great things can we do together?
- How can you perpetuate lifetime values?

Source: James M. Hodge, vice chair and director of principal gifts, Mayo Clinic. Reprinted with permission.

GIVING BENEFITS DONORS

True donor partnerships are both synergistic and symbiotic. Donors participate to advance the mission and benefit the community. Donors also benefit from giving, not in a tangible, quid pro quo sense, but through a variety of positive effects that enhance their quality of life. Research shows that individuals who report high charitable giving also report being physically and mentally healthier (Schwartz et al. 2003) and happier (Brooks 2007) than non-donors and occasional donors. Donors also report achieving self-fulfillment or self-actualization as a result of participating in enabling work that is an extension of their values. For all these reasons, donor relationships are noble partnerships and must be handled with care, integrity, and authenticity. The fund development organization must never forget that donors choose to be the life-breath of the institution's work and to enable the good the organization has in mind.

IN SUMMARY

The reasons donors enter into relationships with healthcare organizations vary, but all reflect their personal values and beliefs. Donors also seek such relationships out of a keen desire to make a tangible impact on other people. To facilitate donor engagement in the work of the healthcare organization, fund development organizations use a variety of tools to focus their time and other resources and to create communications that resonate with donors. These tools must be used with utmost care and respect, and integrity must be the consistent thread running through the relationship. Ultimately, the objective is to create a meaningful, mutually rewarding partnership that benefits the healthcare organization, the donor, and the community.

TWO STEPS TO CREATING A PLATFORM FOR PERFORMANCE

1. **Make donors the heart of the organization.** Discuss your philosophy on nurturing authentic, meaningful, and ethical relationships with donors. Many great resources on creating a donor-centered organization are available. See how the opportunities you find can work hand in hand with your organization's history, culture, and traditions to weave a standard of practice that maintains relationships for a lifetime.

2. **Discuss the use of screening tools.** Decide if you will use screening services that identify wealth, lifestyle, or propensity to give. If so, to what specific and actionable use will they be deployed? What data will be kept, and how can you ensure the security of this information? What guidelines will you put in place to ensure it is used appropriately?

How Do Healthcare Donors Choose Where to Give?

A national survey using hundreds of hours of interviews and research drilled into healthcare donors' methods of choosing an organization to support. It found

- 60 percent visit healthcare organizations' websites,
- 54 percent search the Internet for information,
- 41 percent talk to a donor friend,
- 35 percent check watchdog reports, and
- 29 percent talk to organization staff.

This insight means healthcare organizations need to

- optimize their online presence as a critical communication vehicle,
- demonstrate organizational management/efficiency, and
- engage existing donors to attract new donors.

Source: Russ Reid (2010).

CHAPTER 11

Inviting Donors to Become Partners

Step aside and let the cause walk in.

—*Henry A. Rosso, founder,*
The Fund Raising School

THE ACT OF asking a prospective donor to make a gift may inspire trepidation in even the most committed advocate. Reasons range from

- concern about "doing it right" to
- fear of imposing on someone whose relationship is valued to
- worry that the prospective donor will make a reciprocal request for another cause.

It is time to set aside these obstacles and position the call as the noble work it is: inviting someone to play a fundamental role in an important endeavor.

The commonly held truism for success in fund development is having all the right elements come together: the right solicitor asking the right prospect for the right amount for the right project at the right time. Ensuring the call is made by someone the prospective donor respects and at a convenient time is part of the diligent preparation leading to the auspicious day of the visit. The actual call is about the CAUSE, each letter representing an element of the entreaty:

- **C**ase: A primary purpose of the visit is to articulate the case for support: the proposed solution, the need it would address, the impact it would have, the way it aligns with the healthcare organization's mission/vision/strategy, and the organization's unique ability to champion the project. The case for support is the linchpin of the call and the rationale for community investment.
- **A**dvocacy: Allies on a call have a powerful opportunity to be advocates. Board members gain tremendous credibility by sharing their conviction and passion for the proposed initiative and the value it would have for the community. Advocacy inspires confidence in a prospective donor about the rightness of the work.
- **U**nderstanding: Active listening during the visit enables those on the call to understand a prospective donor's values, hopes, and intent. Open-ended questions should be used to allow a prospective donor to express her thoughts and share how the initiative does—or does not—align with her desire to do good. In a face-to-face visit, the call team interacts with the prospective donor and observes her body language to assess whether the partnership would be a suitable fit.
- **S**tory: Members of the call team must take the opportunity a visit presents to share a story of a real person whose life has been touched or saved. Sharing a story puts a human face on the initiative and helps the prospective donor emotionally connect with the work.
- **E**xample: Words are more compelling when they are rooted in the speaker's actions. Visits with prospective donors are opportunities for members of the call team to set an example. Words are even more resonant when a solicitor says "join me." Disclosure that call team members have made thoughtful gifts commensurate with their financial abilities shows the

prospective donor that they have done what they are asking others to do.

It is a privilege to share the urgent and compelling cause of a healthcare organization. The aim of the solicitor is to share the organization's mission and the case for support without distraction. The solicitor can be confident that while no exchange of material value or quid pro quo occurs when someone makes a gift, donors do receive benefits in return. They are inspired and transformed by making an enabling gift that expresses their values and beliefs and puts them to action. This chapter explores tools and processes that help allies and advocates ask for gifts with confidence and conviction.

SECURING THE VISIT

Setting an appointment with a prospective donor can be the most challenging part of the cultivation and solicitation process. While donors give gladly and gain fulfillment through their actions, some are still reticent to receive a visit, perhaps out of apprehension about the callers' expectations. Others have already determined the level at which they wish to participate and do not want to be asked to contribute more than that amount. For these and other reasons, confirming a date for the visit is a momentous step in the process.

When phoning a potential donor to set an appointment, the caller should focus on communicating the purpose of the visit. For example, the caller might say, "I hope to talk with you about a valuable project I've been working on for [name of the healthcare organization]. I feel it would provide real benefit to our community, and I believe it would interest you." Many people will respond to this statement by asking the caller if the reason for the visit is to ask them for money. Integrity reigns supreme, so the caller's answer should be honest but enthusiastic—for example: "Yes, I am. I hope once you know the details of this project, you will want to join me in helping to make it happen. However, I also want to get your thoughts on our plans and your ideas for making this project successful."

Some will tell the caller not to take the time to visit but rather tell them about the project over the phone—but the purpose of the call is not to state the case or ask for a gift; it is simply to set the appointment. It is important to meet face-to-face and have a genuine two-way dialogue. A personal visit is also a more dignified, respectful way to ask a prospective partner to take on a leadership role in the effort. Finally, other allies can accompany the caller on a visit to provide credibility or information that might convince a donor to participate.

The following are a few objectives for the phone call:

- **Keep small talk to a minimum.** Be cordial and make the person comfortable, but do not distract from the intent of the call.
- **Ask for a 45-minute meeting.** By requesting 45 minutes, you convey that you have a substantial case to make yet will not tie up an entire one-hour block on the person's calendar.
- **Suggest a private location.** It is ideal to meet at the healthcare organization so you can show the donor the facility. Alternatively, meet at the donor's home or office or wherever the donor feels most comfortable. Restaurants and other public places might be distracting or make the person uncomfortable because others may overhear or interrupt your conversation.
- **Include all the decision makers.** Meet with all who would be involved in or affected by the decision to give so they can hear the organization's vision firsthand and make a joint decision. For example, most couples make financial decisions, including decisions about charitable giving, together.
- **Have your calendar ready.** Many people make phone calls while driving or otherwise in motion and cannot easily check their calendars. Be prepared with your schedule and know the availability of others on the visitation team when you make the phone call so you can confirm a time immediately.

Once the appointment has been set, it is ideal to send the person a quick note to thank him and to confirm the date, time, and location of the meeting.

SHORE UP THE SOLICITATION TEAM

Once the in-person visit is secured, the next step is to coordinate the team selected to make the visit. Team members must have a common set of knowledge and a clear plan for who will handle certain aspects of the call.

Brush Up on Background

It is essential for the call team to affirm that everyone is on the same page prior to the call. To make an informed, confident call, the team needs to address the following points:

- Make sure everyone going on the call has a common understanding of the case for support, the community impact of the project, the total cost, the portion of the total cost to be funded by charitable gifts, and the gift amount to be requested from the prospective donor. This information and a proposal can be assembled by the development office.
- Share relevant and appropriate information about the prospective donor with the team so everyone is familiar with his interests, financial ability, and other elements that might incline him to give—for example:
  —When the person made his first, last, and largest gift
  —Projects or services he supported in the past
  —His connection to the organization (e.g., grateful patient)
  —Potential conflicts: whether he has family, business, or other commitments

Exercise discretion when sharing information with team members or saving information in a file or donor database. Never disclose or store information that would embarrass, hurt, or otherwise harm a prospective donor if it were shared.

- Ensure that everyone is aware of any relationships the prospective donor has with call team members. For example, he may have been high school friends with a call team member, attended the same church, or shared business interests. This background information helps team members determine who would be most credible to the donor and thus best positioned to ask for a gift.

Define Team Roles

Members of the call team play various roles during the visit. The specific responsibilities of each participant should be established in advance. The team will approach the call with more focus and assurance if each person clearly understands what he is supposed to do. The following roles are common personas team members assume on a call:

- **The visionary:** The CEO usually fulfills this role. She explains the organization's ambitions, positions the organization as uniquely qualified to advance the plan, describes the impact the project would have on the community, and so forth. The presence of the CEO also inspires confidence in the organization's ability to execute its plans.
- **The (impartial) advocate:** A board member of either the foundation or the hospital generally provides credibility. He conveys genuine passion for the cause and expresses why he thinks it merits community investment. The board volunteer clearly derives no personal financial benefit from an investment in the organization and thus represents the value of the cause to advancing the greater good. The board member is often a primary connection to the prospective donor

and has earned the prospective donor's respect and confidence. For all these reasons, board members often ask for the gift.

- **The expert:** A physician typically explains the clinical merit of the case. She shares the initiative's potential to enhance medical capabilities, improve treatment and outcomes, and ultimately touch people's lives. The physician is a trusted, credible authority who is seen more as an advocate for patients than as an agent of the organization. She adds even more value to the visit when the prospective donor is a grateful patient with whom she has a relationship.

- **The technician:** A development staff member generally assists with details. For example, he shares pledge periods, recognition opportunities, various financial methods of making a gift, and so forth. The staff member should also be well-versed in the case and able to answer any questions others may not be in a position to answer. This person also picks up other tasks if inadvertently other team members do not fully deliver.

Agree on Who Will Ask for the Gift

Another key decision to make in advance is selection of the team member who will ask for the gift. If this decision is not made prior to the call, team members often fritter away time during the visit, each waiting for someone else to ask.

MAKING THE SOLICITATION CALL

Solicitation calls have a common rhythm that becomes palpable to call team members after they have been on a few visits. The following stages are part of this predictable progression:

- **Settle: Talk about mutual interests to make everyone comfortable.** When the call team arrives, handshakes and hellos are exchanged and everyone is ushered into an area to sit. The visit starts with light conversation on subjects of mutual interest. This preamble should not last so long that the potential donor starts to feel impatient that the team has not come to the point of the visit and the social conversation consumes too much of the time needed to explain the case.

- **Open: "Thanks for taking the time to visit with us. Here's the reason for our call."** Generally, the ally the prospective donor most respects and likely knows best—often the board member—opens the business conversation. He thanks her for her time and proceeds by expressing that the reason for the call is to share information on a project of great importance in the community and potentially of interest to her.

  Most calls are made to people who have participated as donors in the past, so at this point in the conversation the group often has an opportunity to acknowledge the donor's past history with the organization and ask her why she made her first gift. This question takes the donor back to when the gift was made and gives her a chance to share the circumstances that made it happen and the values she expressed through her gift. This recollection reminds the donor of her past reasons for giving and reaffirms her convictions about the cause. It also helps inform the solicitation team of the motivations that have driven the donor's past involvement. When visiting someone who has not given before, the team can ask open-ended questions to explore the person's values, motivations, and interest in the organization.

- **Case: Share the solution/opportunity and its potential impact.** A member of the call team—typically the CEO, the board member, or a physician, depending on who is best positioned to tell the story and how many are on the call team—shares the case for support. He explains the proposed initiative, the impact it is expected to have, project costs, and financing plans. The case for support should be illustrated by a story that shows the impact this initiative would have on a single person so the donor can relate to the project. (See Chapter 9 for more detail on storytelling.)

Next, the thread of the rationale for the project is typically passed among the team members. For example, the physician adds her clinical assessment of the value added by the project, and the board member expresses his personal belief that the project adds genuine value to the community.

Team members also elicit the prospective donor's input at this point in the conversation through open-ended questions and assess from her reactions and comments the degree of alignment between her objectives and the project. The purpose of this dialogue is to gain insights into the donor's intent and objectives and to uncover opportunities to add value to the project. In most cases, the team would not have made the visit without already anticipating the prospective donor's baseline interests.

- **Ask: Ask the person to consider giving a specific amount.** Following the dialogue just described, it is time to ask for the gift. As a lead-up, the commitment of others, including board members, employees, physicians, and call team members, may be shared. Most often the board member or CEO presents the question, stating, for example, "I hope you will consider [joining me in] being part of this project to advance the healing work of [the healthcare organization]. Would you consider making a gift in the range of [dollar amount]?"
- **Pause: Give the prospective donor time to think.** She has a lot to weigh in her mind:
  —Does this initiative align with my values and aspirations for giving?
  —Does this request synch with my charitable priorities at this time?
  —Does this particular project accomplish what I want to do?

—What other financial and charitable commitments do I have or expect?

—Is this amount one I can afford to give and want to give?

—What will I potentially have to give up to make this commitment?

—What else is going on in my life that I need to prepare for: child's college tuition, child's wedding expenses, new business opportunity, retirement?

—Would making this gift compromise the financial resources I feel I need to maintain my safety, security, or lifestyle?

This pause is almost always an awkward moment. The silence is uncomfortable. Team members will feel pressured to say something, but they should be quiet and do whatever it takes to remain so (e.g., count silently to 20, drink some water). The next words uttered should be the prospective donor's.

- **Respond: Answer questions or objections.** People who are asked to make major financial decisions generally want to ensure they fully understand the details, so most either pose an objection or ask a question at this point. Some might even say no. The following responses are common objections call teams encounter:

—"I am concerned about the economy."

—"Don't tax dollars support [name of healthcare organization]?"

—"I don't understand why [name of healthcare organization] needs philanthropy."

—"I need to talk to my spouse before considering a financial commitment."

—"I need to think about it" or "I'm not prepared to decide now."

—"I'm not able to make a gift at this time/of this size."

—"Small charities need my help more than [name of healthcare organization] does."

The call team listens patiently and attentively until the prospective donor fully expresses his feelings or concerns. In response, the person who posed the original question restates the objection and empathizes with the person. For example, one might say, "I hear you when you say [objection], and I understand why it's an important consideration." The call team member respectfully proceeds by answering the concern and provides relevant information.

In his beautifully articulated article "Fundraising's Four Magic Questions" (reprinted in part in this chapter), author and consultant Jerold Panas talks about exploring a prospective donor's objections through four key questions:

—Is it the organization?
—Is it the specific project?
—Is it the amount?
—Is it the timing?

He recommends probing in these four areas to find out what the root of a prospective donor's concern is so it can be addressed.

After acknowledging and addressing the prospective donor's concern, the team member restates the gift request in a way that accommodates the concern—for example, "I am glad we had an opportunity to openly discuss your questions and concerns. If you feel those issues have been answered to your satisfaction, might you consider joining us in advancing this project through a gift in the range of [gift amount]?"

- **Exit: Leave on a positive note, no matter the outcome.** The call ends with gracious thanks whether the answer was yes or no. If the answer was no, the team can ask the person if she is amenable to another visit in the future or invite her to visit the healthcare organization when conditions are more ideal. If the answer was yes, the team confirms that a mutual understanding has been reached and addresses any other needs the donor might have.

Panas's Four Magic Questions

We had come to that charged moment—frightening and awesome, when the air crackles with hope and expectation. The time had come . . . I was about to ask Dick for his gift . . .

The visit had gone mostly as planned. But, no matter how often you've asked for a gift, thoughts race through your mind before you speak those magic words: Did I probe enough? Do I really know Dick's primary interest? Did I talk enough about the benefits and how his gift would change lives? Am I asking for the right amount? . . .

I present the opportunity . . .

I would like you to consider a gift of $100,000 that will save lives for a generation to come and transform this into one of the great cardiac centers of the country. The words "I would like you to consider" are the ones I find most appropriate.

Ah, I've asked for the gift. That wasn't so difficult after all.

Pause.

I follow the example I teach others. Make the ask, and for a precise amount. Don't fill in the silence. No matter how long it may seem, wait. Follow the dictum: The first one who speaks is dead! And so I pause . . . for what seems eternity. Dick finally responds.

No, I don't think so, he says . . .

Perhaps you're thinking it's time you gather your things . . .

Wrong!

→

You've only come to the *beginning* of your ask . . .

I must find out whether Dick responded the way he did because:

1. There's no great feeling or involvement with the institution.
2. There is a lack of interest in the specific project.
3. I asked for too much.
4. The timing is a factor.

I must know the answer to these immutable questions: Is it the organization, the project, the amount, or the timing? And I mustn't leave until I do . . .

Dick, I said, thanks for responding so clearly to my request. And I did hear what you said. I don't mean to press you on the matter . . . but I feel I must ask you a question. . . . Is there something that bothers you about the hospital? You've been a supporter for so long . . . Do you still feel that same friendship and support?

Oh, yes, Dick said. . . . I think they're doing a great job. (I'm past the first hurdle.)

I continued.

I was pretty sure you felt that way. I also sensed this was the kind of project that would really interest you . . . Is there something about the project that makes you hesitate?

Oh, no. Certainly not, Dick says. On the contrary, the Center is something I feel is very important . . .

(Great! . . . [N]ow to the really tough question. If I get by this one, we have the gift.)

→

... Dick, did I ask for too much? ... I honestly felt that based on your ... past support, $100,000 was just about the amount you'd want to give to a program this important ...

Dick responds: No, you were correct, that's just about the amount I'd like to give to a project like this. (Yea! This was working out better than I could have hoped ...)

And now, my final question.

Is it the timing, Dick? Is the timing off? ...

That's it exactly, said Dick ... [H]e went on to explain how it would be impossible to make a gift, even a small one, at this time ... [T]here simply weren't funds available ...

But that's the easiest part of all ... Let's extend the timing.

Source: This excerpt is drawn from Jerold Panas's (2003) book, *Asking: A 59-Minute Guide to Everything Board Members, Volunteers, and Staff Need to Know to Secure the Gift,* published by Emerson & Church (www.emersonandchurch). Used with permission.

Gracious Thanks

The art of the "ask" is followed by the art of the thank-you. It is important to thank donors often, creatively, and graciously. After a gift commitment is secured, the team might feel the process is done. However, the opposite is true for the donor: The gift commitment is just the beginning. From this point, the richness of the relationship unfolds as the donor sees how the organization handles the relationship and advances the proposed plans. Organizations have an opportunity to build lifelong relationships during this time and should pay as much attention to stewarding as it did to asking for the gift.

Thanking Is as Important as Asking

It is important to tell donors that their gift is making a real impact and is appreciated. Here are some ideas for meaningful, mission-centered thank-yous that will help organizations retain donors:

1. Handwritten thank-you note from the CEO/board member/physician
2. Thank-you card signed by clinical staff or patients
3. Before-and-after pictures of an improvement funded by the donor's gift (e.g., renovated hospital unit)
4. Naming a room or an area of the organization after the donor
5. Behind-the-scenes tour
6. Invitation to meet with key physicians involved in the project
7. Invitation to attend grand rounds in the donor's area of interest
8. Involvement in focus groups
9. Publicity of various types
10. Invitation to communicate to employees/the board the reason for the gift (orally or in writing)
11. Involvement in planning and other functions for the area funded by the gift
12. Invitations to events celebrating giving or program success

IN SUMMARY

Asking someone to be part of a healthcare organization's healing work is a noble endeavor. The time invested in visits to prospective donors is used well if the call team focuses on the CAUSE: case, advocacy, understanding, story, and example. These visits are vital opportunities to turn valuable relationships into partnerships in which organizations and donors stand shoulder-to-shoulder to advance a common vision.

THREE STEPS TO CREATING A PLATFORM FOR PERFORMANCE

1. **Give them the tools.** Community leadership volunteers and healthcare executives are generally accustomed to success, so give them the tools they need to be successful. Train them in the art of solicitation. Walk them through what they should expect on a call. Help them find their words, both to tell the story and to handle objections. Have them participate in mock calls so they gain experience and become adept at communicating the rationale for giving.

2. **Use your personal power.** If fear or nervousness has stopped you from participating in a direct solicitation role in the past, make a deal with yourself to go on at least three visits this year. On the first call, you may struggle to find the right words or feel uncomfortable, but by the third time you will likely experience the joy of building partnerships. Rather than hesitating to participate, you'll be asking to go on visits.

3. **Create a success zone.** Ask allies who are still reticent to go on calls to consider visiting with their peers on the medical staff or on the executive team—people they know and feel comfortable with. Have them shadow an experienced peer. Send them on calls to steady donors and good friends you already know are a "yes." Give them a chance to "test their wings" in a safe and friendly environment.

CHAPTER 12

Driving Excellence
Through Evaluation

A culture of discipline is not a principle of business;
it is a principle of greatness.

—Jim Collins

HEALTHCARE PHILANTHROPY IS an integral part of funding
the advancement of the healthcare organization, so rigor must be
applied to ensure it functions and delivers at its level of potential.

Inside the organization, solid evaluation based on fund development metrics and other key performance indicators gauges current
success against potential by quantifying effectiveness and identifying
opportunities for improvement. Donors invest in organizations that
achieve results, so diligent and continued evaluation to demonstrate
effectiveness is becoming an expectation. Donors have observed poor
management practices in other charitable organizations through the
media, and they want increased transparency and stronger accountability. A 2003 article in *Nonprofit Quarterly* shared, "Like it or
not, charity watchdogs are becoming increasingly popular with the
information-hungry public, and the financial ratios they employ are
now being accepted as proxies for performance, quality and integrity" (Lammers 2003). By gathering information through evaluation
and making it public, an organization demonstrates accountability
and stewardship to organizational donors and gains their trust.

CONFRONTING EVALUATION PROBLEMS

While appropriate evaluation is a significant means of enabling performance, it poses problems that must be confronted. Many ratios used by charity watchdogs and some charitable organizations themselves are fundamentally flawed because of rampant inconsistences in reporting, cost allocation, and valuation. Because most comparisons have been "apples to oranges," their validity is questionable.

Definition Problems

The nonprofit industry is rife with definition problems, in part because the Financial Accounting Standards Board and the Internal Revenue Service (IRS) offer limited guidance on counting and allocating revenues and expenses. For example, when a foundation counts organizational revenues, does it count just cash, or cash and pledges? Does it use the current value or net present value of those revenues? Does it book revocable gifts? Lacking clear direction, charitable organizations have considerable leeway in interpretation and accounting. Two organizations in the same circumstances could calculate costs and returns differently through equally appropriate means and report divergent outcomes as a result.

The definition problem continues with the assignment of expenses to different categories of use. For example, when healthcare foundations distribute a magazine that includes health and wellness information but also a return envelope in which recipients can enclose a gift, some would allocate the publication to *program expense* because the health information could further the charitable mission by providing consumer education, while others would count the publication as a *fundraising expense* because it contains a solicitation. Neither approach is wrong; definition is simply lacking.

Healthcare foundations have traditionally been in a unique situation with regard to indirect expenses. For example, many healthcare organizations employ the foundation staff and "loan" them to the foundation, so salaries and benefits are not a direct expense of the foundation organization. Healthcare organizations also provide other overhead benefits, such as office space, information technology, and accounting services.

A quote from a presentation at an Association for Healthcare Philanthropy regional conference sums up the issue of expense allocation: "When asked by a CEO 'What is our fundraising cost?' I ask, 'What do you want it to be?'" (Erickson, McGinly, and Steinke 2009). Without rigid definition of how costs should be treated, they are fungible. Any number of expenses can be allocated as either costs of the foundation or costs of the hospital or can be attributed as fundraising costs or program expenses. While the IRS seeks to remedy some of these inconsistencies through Form 990 for charitable reporting, foundations largely have not considered significant in-kind contributions from the healthcare organization when determining the cost of fundraising.

Beyond accounting policies and cost allocation, lack of definition of the foundation's role has caused reporting discrepancies in total dollars raised. For example, some healthcare foundations count only grant dollars generated by philanthropy through private foundations, corporate foundations, community foundations, and family foundations, while other foundations count philanthropic grants **and** governmental grants, dramatically increasing the reported total dollars raised. Again, neither interpretation is rooted in bad faith.

Bad Data

Another issue is inaccurate data that are self-reported by charitable organizations in their IRS filings and readily available through such websites as Guidestar.org. Charitable efficiency ratios are generally calculated using information from IRS 990 filings, and these filings do not always paint a fair, consistent picture of the impact or effectiveness of an organization. Sargeant and Shang (2010) state that "almost 60 percent of nonprofit organizations claim to have zero fundraising costs," and according to Gregory and Howard (2009), "[O]ne in eight reported no management or general expenses." While some small, volunteer-led organizations relying solely on personal solicitation may legitimately have little or no fundraising expenses, self-reported data are unlikely to be an accurate portrayal of cost.

Realistic Expectations

An issue closely related to bad data is having realistic expectations for what fundraising should cost. Ann Goggins Gregory, director of knowledge management for a nonprofit strategy consulting firm, and colleague Don Howard point out, "Many funders know nonprofit organizations report artificially low overhead figures and that donor literature often reflects grossly inaccurate program ratios (the ratio of program-related expenses to indirect expenses). Without accurate data, funders do not know what overhead rates *should be*" (Gregory and Howard 2009).

Donors also may have unrealistic expectations. According to Gregory and Howard (2009), a 2001 survey by the Better Business Bureau's Wise Giving Alliance found that more than half of American adults feel nonprofits' overhead should be 20 percent or less of total spending. Those surveyed said overhead ratios are more important than the success of the organization's programs. The authors observe that nonprofit organizations feel such tremendous pressure to keep overhead low that "[a] vicious cycle is leaving nonprofits so hungry for decent infrastructure that they can barely function as organizations—let alone serve their beneficiaries." At the same time, they continue to underreport costs to fulfill funders' and donors' expectation that they be diligent stewards.

Lots of Correlated Variables

Performance may also be legitimately influenced by a range of factors that are largely uncontrollable, both ongoing and at particular points in the foundation life cycle. Appropriate performance for an organization depends on its unique circumstances. For example,

---

It Takes Money to Make Money

Financial investment is required to build and sustain a fund development program. While enduring relationships can be built with tools as simple as a telephone call and a handshake, successful development efforts invest in systems and infrastructure, such as

- capacity-building programs for acquiring first-time donors (while financial return on investment may be low, engaging new donors is critical);
- information systems for managing donor information;
- programs, such as wealth screening, for optimizing efficiency;
- tools, such as communications, for stewarding and retaining donors;
- high-value, smart growth programs, such as planned giving, that do not yield immediate cash flow but offer tremendous long-term potential; and
- professional memberships, education, and certification that drive excellence and keep development teams on the leading edge of emerging practice and legislation.

An organization that builds a well-rounded, well-grounded program supported by the right infrastructure and run by professional staff sets the stage to deliver increasing results over the long term.

---

the prevalently used "cost to raise a dollar" ratio is affected by a range of highly correlated variables that can dramatically influence evaluation of fundraising performance. These variables include

- appeal of the mission (e.g., long-term care versus children's hospital),
- life cycle stage of the development effort (e.g., emerging versus well-established),
- foundation staffing (e.g., one generalist versus 20 specialists),
- organization size (e.g., small rural center versus major academic center),
- profile of patients served (e.g., largely Medicaid versus largely commercial),
- types of fund development undertaken (e.g., events versus major gifts),
- donor acquisition/development (e.g., capacity building versus growth), and
- brand appeal (e.g., community hospital versus national academic leader).

Cautions About Enterprise-Level Data

An extension of accounting for correlated variables is recognizing that efficiency metrics that look at the entire fund development enterprise may be less meaningful for comparison if limiting factors are in play. For example, a common metric for overall program evaluation is the "cost per dollar raised," which shows how efficiently the fund development organization raised its dollars. This number is calculated by dividing total expenses by gross revenues and then multiplying by 100 to move the decimal point. While different studies report slightly different numbers, the Association for Healthcare Philanthropy (2011b) reports that the cost to raise a dollar has been hovering around 30 cents (33 cents in fiscal year 2010).

While this number is an excellent check for efficiency and performance, it may cover up both efficiencies and inefficiencies at the individual program level. For example, this number can change materially—especially in a smaller program—by the impact of a few outsize major or planned gifts. The number is also affected by program mix, which is often largely attributable to the life cycle stage of the program. For example, a young development program building capacity through a heavy mix of donor acquisition programs may have a disproportionate share of direct mail costs (which often run close to a dollar to raise a dollar) and a small number of major gifts representing low costs to raise a dollar. In this situation, the low-cost share would not offset/balance the overall number to the degree that it would in a program whose costs are more evenly distributed because it is at a more advanced stage. In contrast, a mature program with deep relationships likely benefits from a steady stream of major and planned gifts that represent low costs to raise a dollar. Though the development leaders at the early and later stages both may be running effective programs, their numbers might look vastly different because of the differences in life cycle stage and program mix.

Patience Is Key to Success

A strong healthcare fund development effort makes a considerable impact over the long haul. Time and investment are required to build a program that fulfills its potential. For example, it often takes five or more years to get traction in a major gifts program and as many as ten years to build a vibrant planned-giving program. In the interim, an organization's success at raising enough dollars to accomplish its mission objectives may be a better gauge of program value than efficiency.

> ### *Balancing Future Capacity Against Present Dollars*
>
> Development programs have different requirements for building capacity and different abilities to generate income from philanthropic dollars at different points in their life cycle. The following is a quick overview of efforts that fall under each category:
>
> **Capacity-Building Programs**
> - Infrastructure creation (e.g., data management system)
> - Operating expenses (e.g., staff)
> - New-donor acquisition programs (e.g., direct mail)
> - Public relations (e.g., donor newsletter)
> - Stewardship programs (e.g., donor recognition wall)
> - Prospect research (e.g., wealth screening)
>
> **Income-Creating Programs**
> - Donor gift renewal (e.g., annual fund)
> - Special events (e.g., gala)
> - Major gifts (e.g., personal solicitation)
> - Planned giving (e.g., bequest program)
> - Capital campaign (e.g., major building campaign)
> - Grants (e.g., foundation gifts)
>
> ---
>
> *Source:* Adapted from Levis (1993).

STILL, CLEAR VALUE IN MEASUREMENT

Despite the challenges that organizations must be conscious of when creating an evaluation plan, appropriate measurement has clear value. As Jim Collins (2005) said in his monograph *Good to Great and the Social Sectors*, "To throw up our hands and say, 'But, we cannot measure performance in the social sectors the way you can in business' is simply a lack of discipline. All indicators are flawed, whether qualitative or quantitative. Test scores are flawed. Mammograms are flawed, crime data are flawed, customer service data are flawed. What matters is not finding the perfect indicator, but settling upon a consistent and intelligent method of assessing your output results."

The White Knights of Philanthropy Benchmarking

Organizations have allies in their quest to achieve meaningful evaluation. The Association for Healthcare Philanthropy established its Performance Benchmarking Service in 2003, and the Advisory Board Company's Philanthropy Leadership Council developed a similar service in 2005. Both efforts are exclusively dedicated to benchmarking philanthropy specific to healthcare organizations. More important, both have rigorous definitions for all revenue and expense categories to ensure apples-to-apples comparisons. Both enable participant organizations to produce reports to compare their progress to similar organizations (e.g., those with similar staff size, similar size of operations, or a similar number of years in major gifts fundraising). A well-designed, well-maintained service of this caliber can be a valuable tool for setting right-sized aspirations and expectations for philanthropy. The Association for Healthcare Philanthropy's service publishes two reports annually that include an analysis of the data; the cost of participation is about $1,000 annually plus a membership that costs about $500 annually and a onetime benchmarking setup fee. The Advisory Board Company's service gives members access to real-time (continuously updated) data through an online portal; the service is included with annual membership, which runs about $25,000 annually. While other firms that provide general benchmarking services for healthcare offer data on philanthropy, the quality of the data does not rise to the level of that offered by the Association for Healthcare Philanthropy and the Advisory Board Company in part because of the rigor of the definitions and processes these two services use.

Evaluation for Impact

Healthcare foundations can also use internal metrics to evaluate efforts or programs. It is important that metrics selected for this purpose (W. K. Kellogg Foundation 2004)

- highlight areas the foundation can largely control (e.g., number of face-to-face visits);
- capture cause–effect relationships (e.g., number of proposals presented);
- drill activity that involves execution (e.g., number of calls with an ally);
- force proactive planning (e.g., number of prospects with research profiles);
- focus measurement on the most valued tasks; and
- consider inputs, outputs, and outcomes.

The only caveat in internal benchmarking efforts is that comparison of one's performance to its past performance presents its own set of problems. For example, an organization that sees a trend of growth or improvement might be benchmarking against past mediocrity or subpar results. Therefore, if an organization takes this approach to evaluation, it is essential that it set its ambitions against some external data points to ensure their appropriateness. For example, it might research the cost of operating particular programs, the anticipated rates of response to particular programs, and so forth.

Evaluate at a Level That Makes the Most Sense

The most meaningful evaluation of fund development happens at the program level, where the performance of each activity is measured. For example, one could consider the performance of a specific program (e.g., annual giving) or a specific appeal of that program (e.g., fall direct-mail acquisition campaign). This approach eliminates issues with enterprise-level data that do not account for program mix; the more granular the data, the more meaningful they become. However, again, a caveat is that even program-level data are influenced by such elements as average gift size, so program maturity and similar issues still come into play and necessitate consideration of the context/environment in which the organization is operating. When the fund development organization evaluates its programs individually rather than together as a whole, it can decide which specific program elements are performing at their expectations, what needs attention, what should be continued, what merits additional investment, and so forth.

A variety of metrics at the program level capture leading or lagging indicators of success, including

- all programs: total dollars raised (lagging),
- all programs: cost of raising each dollar (lagging),
- all programs: number of new/returning/recovered donors (lagging),
- all programs: flat/increasing/decreasing donor gift size (lagging),
- all programs: response rate to the appeal (lagging),
- all programs: average gift size (lagging),
- major gifts: prospects under active management (leading),
- major gifts: number of face-to-face visits made (leading),
- major gifts: number of visits with key ally assist (leading),
- major gifts: proposals presented (leading),
- major gifts: proposals accepted/gift made (lagging),
- major gifts: fulfillment rate on pledges (lagging), and
- planned giving: gift expectancies (leading).

External benchmarks, which are available for most of these metrics, enable the organization to determine whether its program is performing at a level commensurate with peer programs.

It can be difficult to break down operating expenses to determine the cost allocation to programs for items such as staff time, administrative costs (e.g., for data management), and other overhead costs, but by doing so one can gain better insight into the merit of some programs. For example, an organization may think one of its special events is performing at the typical cost to raise a dollar of about 50 cents because it spent $50,000 to raise $100,000. However, the organization has considered only direct costs in the calculation. Once it attributes the cost of staff salaries and employee benefits associated with the event, it may add another, say, $25,000 of overhead cost. Inclusion of this amount increases the cost to raise each dollar to 75 cents and makes the fundraising merits of continuing the event questionable.

Finding Current Benchmarking Data

Benchmarking data on charitable programs, both specific to healthcare and nonspecific, are available from several sources. Performance numbers have fluctuated in recent years as programs increase their professionalism, efficiency, and effectiveness on one side of the equation but continue to receive a beating from the economy on the other. Thus, it is best to look for the latest available numbers to ensure you are comparing your work to the most relevant data available. Some sources include

- Association for Healthcare Philanthropy (healthcare specific),
- Advisory Board Company (healthcare specific),
- publications by James M. Greenfield (healthcare specific),
- Association of Fundraising Professionals (all nonprofit sectors),
- National Center for Charitable Statistics (all nonprofit sectors), and
- Center on Philanthropy at Indiana University (all nonprofit sectors).

Focus on What Matters

Organizations also need to focus on and measure what matters. An adaptation of an anecdote shared by Jim Collins (2005) in *Good to Great and the Social Sectors* illustrates this point: What's more important to you: to have the most **efficient** team in NCAA Division I college football by having the lowest-paid coach, whose salary runs about $200,000, or to have the most **effective** team (the most wins), even if the coach is paid $5 million? While everyone wants to see organizations run efficiently, folks who are painting their faces and holding up foam fingers to cheer on their team probably care a lot more about the outcome of the game than about the cost of conducting it. Organizations need to select metrics based on the results they want to achieve, and the objective may not be to spend as little as possible but to raise as much as possible.

While a lot of benchmarking efforts focus on resource utilization and returns, thought leaders believe that evaluation should focus on the following instead:

- **Outcomes** that show whether the organization is accomplishing what it set out to do (How does it define success, and is it achieving it?)
- **Leading indicators** that tend to predict future performance and outcomes (Instead of waiting until an activity or a process is completed to look at results, evaluate actions at the front end of the process that are known to lead to desired outcomes.)

The Ultimate Leading Indicators

In fund development, two "ultimate" leading indicators drive outcomes:

- Donor engagement
- Engagement of allies, including board members, executives, and physicians

Jim Greenfield (2005), a respected leader in fund development evaluation, wisely says that the number of participating donors is "a critical indicator of success; money follows people." One of the best indicators of a thriving program is its ability to attract and proactively advance relationships. Engaged donors who are motivated to build long-term relationships with the organization are key to securing charitable funds.

Likewise, the engagement of senior executives, board members, physicians, and other key allies is the heart of the healthcare philanthropy effort. These advocates provide critical connections, create a broad network of donors, and infuse the effort with credibility. If the fund development organization concentrates on engaging these key enablers, it will achieve all the other metrics and the excellence to which it aspires.

IN SUMMARY

Fund development is a relationship-based discipline shaped by art and science and honed by establishing quantitative metrics and replicating best practices. While there are pitfalls to avoid when setting up a meaningful evaluation system, evaluation enables sound management decisions related to program continuation, investment, and adaptation. By implementing an evaluation program, the development organization raises its standards for accountability and signals to the broader healthcare organization that fund development is a core and valued function.

FOUR STEPS TO CREATING A PLATFORM FOR PERFORMANCE

1. **Set the stage.** Select a few metrics for philanthropy to monitor alongside other key performance metrics for the healthcare organization. By doing so, you communicate that you demand

the same level of accountability you demand from operations and signal the importance of philanthropy to achieving the organization's goals.

2. **Choose metrics carefully.** To use benchmarking to guide program evaluation and improvement, you must carefully define the framework for your program, select metrics that uncover both competencies and deficiencies, choose issues appropriate to the program's life cycle stage, and monitor controllable measures that drive key processes.

3. **Right-size your evaluation efforts.** Track enough information to be able to meaningfully evaluate your program but not so much that the organization is drowning in data or devoting too much time to measurement and too little time to advancing relationships.

4. **Find a trusted partner.** Use of a highly structured, healthcare-specific benchmarking service is important for rigorous, meaningful measurement.

Interview with Mark Larkin, CFRE, Executive Director, CentraCare Health Foundation

CentraCare Health System is a not-for-profit healthcare organization of hospitals, clinics, and long-term care facilities serving a mostly rural geographic region of nearly 700,000 people in central Minnesota. CentraCare touches the lives of nearly 150,000 people annually and has gross revenues of nearly $1 billion. The flagship facility based in St. Cloud, Minnesota, is a magnet hospital and has been on the Thomson Reuters 100 Top Hospitals list eight times in the last 12 years and on the Top 100 Heart Hospitals list eight times as well. The foundation raises about $7.2 million dollars annually through philanthropy. Mr. Larkin is the vice president of

→

development for the CentraCare Health System and has more than 25 years of fundraising experience, 15 of which are in healthcare development with CentraCare Health Foundation.

QUESTION: Why did you seek to participate in a robust benchmarking program?

ANSWER: It is part of our organizational culture to focus on quality and cost-effectiveness, and the foundation is no different. Benchmarking helps to set realistic expectations, give confidence in our business planning, and create the baseline to know if we are improving or not. It identifies best practices and helps set objectives for new and current programs.

QUESTION: Can you tell me about a specific change or improvement you have made to your development efforts as a result of participation?

ANSWER: We are setting realistic objectives for our major gift officers. Each year we look at the number of face-to-face visits, number of major gifts solicited, and number of major gifts closed and compare this to organizations with the same budget size as our foundation's. This is just one of the many metrics we use.

QUESTION: How do you feel benchmarking has enhanced your overall efforts to advance philanthropy?

ANSWER: My peers within the organization treat me as a professional. I do not hear the comments that fundraising is "only about parties." My colleagues in the C-suite and in the direct-care field view our staff with great respect,

→

and they know we follow a solid business plan, just like the operations staff do. Our board members state we are "the best, most professional nonprofit in this regional community"; that quote came from our board chair, a CPA of a large accounting firm. He made that comment shortly after making a six-figure gift to our organization.

QUESTION: If you had advice for healthcare CEOs on the importance of evaluation and benchmarking for philanthropy programs, what would it be?

ANSWER: As a CEO, you expect each of your service lines or healthcare business units to have a business plan, and you evaluate what they do based on metrics; why would you not ask the same of your fundraising department?

QUESTION: What else do we need to know?

ANSWER: I have not been able to find third-party data about how the donor relationship will enhance the brand of your healthcare organization. However, if you start and follow the metrics for major gift fundraising in whatever size market you live in, you will be able to study and see a marked improvement in the reputation of your healthcare organization over time. Enhancing the brand of the healthcare organization is difficult, but a strong development staff working with key community leaders in concert with the CEO and senior leadership of the organization will take your brand to new heights in care delivery. Fundraising and major gift fundraising in particular are not about the transaction of making a gift; they are about relationships that build advocates and give your healthcare organization a competitive edge that is difficult to reproduce.

References

Aaker, J., and A. Smith. 2010. *The Dragonfly Effect*. San Francisco: Jossey-Bass.

Advisory Board Company. 2007. "Connecting Through Care: Best Practices in Grateful Patient Fundraising." Accessed June 14. www.advisory.com/Research/ Philanthropy-Leadership-Council/Studies/2007/Connecting-Through-Care.

American College of Healthcare Executives. 2011. "Top Issues Confronting Hospitals: 2010." Published January 24. www.ache.org/Pubs/Releases/2011/ topissues.cfm.

Association for Healthcare Philanthropy. 2011a. "AHP Report on Giving FY2010." Accessed May 3. www.ahp.org/publicationandtools/Documents/AHP_FY2010 Factsheet_US.pdf.

———. 2011b. "Nonprofit Hospitals Raise $8.26 Billion in Donations in FY2010, With Individual Donors the Majority of Pledges, AHP Reports. But Fundraising Costs More in Recession." Published June 13. www.ahp.org/publicationand tools/News/Releases/2011newsrelease/Pages/061311.aspx.

Association of Fundraising Professionals. 2009. "Frequently Asked Questions About Fundraising Ethics." www.afpnet.org/Ethics/EnforcementDetail.cfm? ItemNumber=4013.

Barreda, A. A. 2008. *Historia de un Letrero*. Published June 18. www.youtube .com/watch?v=zyGEEamz7ZM.

Bentz Whaley Flessner. 2011. "11th Annual Healthcare Survey Results." Posted October 13. www.bwf.com/articles/11th-annual-healthcare-survey-results.

———. 2010. "What the Affluent Think About Giving to Healthcare: 2010 Annual Survey." Posted March 10. www.bwf.com/books/what-the-affluent-think-about-giving-to-healthcare.

———. 2009. "What the Affluent Think About Giving to Healthcare: 2009 Annual Survey." Posted April 9. www.bwf.com/books/what-the-affluent-think-about-giving-to-healthcare-2009-annual-survey.

Binder, J., C. Deao, and B. Taylor. 2011. "The Data Is In: Service Excellence Cultivates Giving." *AHP Journal* (spring): 14–23.

Bremer, F. J. 2009. *John Winthrop: Biography as History*. New York: The Continuum International Publishing Group Inc.

Bremner, R. H. 1988. *American Philanthropy*. Chicago: University of Chicago Press.

Brooks, A. C. 2007. "Does Giving Make You Prosperous?" *Journal of Economics and Finance* 31 (3): 403–12.

Cameron, C. D., and B. K. Payne. 2011. "The Emotions of Aid." *Stanford Social Innovation Review* (summer).

Clarke, R. L. 2011. Personal communication, October 17.

Collins, J. 2005. *Good to Great and the Social Sectors.* New York: HarperCollins Publishers.

Conley, M. 2011. "Could You Bill Your Doctor for Making You Wait?" *ABC News.* Published July 7. abcnews.go.com/Health/patients-billed-doctors-waiting-time/story?id=14009452.

Cook, W. B., and W. F. Lasher. 1996. "Toward a Theory of Fundraising in Higher Education." *Review of Higher Education* 20 (1): 33–51.

de Tocqueville, A. 1835. *Democracy in America,* translated by H. Reeve. London: Saunders and Otley.

Erickson, P., W. C. McGinly, and T. Steinke. 2009. "Best Practices in Benchmarking: The Importance of Benchmarking for Progress." Presentation at the Association for Healthcare Philanthropy Midwest Regional Conference, May 17–19.

Fine, P. 2011. Personal communication, October 11.

Frankel, M. 2011. Personal communication, September 20.

Fraser, B. 2010. "Archetypal Stories." Accessed May 3. people.pwf.cam.ac.uk/blf10/Links/stories.html.

Freiherr, G. 2008. "Philips Expands CT Portfolio with 128-Slice Scanner." Published December 2. www.diagnosticimaging.com/conference-reports/rsna2008/business-and-vendors/article/113619/1356044.

Gearon, C. J. 2011. "For Hospitals, a Value Judgment." *U.S. News and World Report.* Published July 18. health.usnews.com/health-news/best-practices-in-health/articles/2011/07/18/for-hospitals-a-value-judgment.

Giving USA Foundation. 2011. "Giving USA 2011." Accessed June 18. www.givingusareports.org.

Goldstein, L. 2011. "Hospital Revenues in Critical Condition." Healthcare Financial Management Association. Accessed May 3. www.hfma.org/Templates/Print.aspx?id=28442.

Greenfield, J. M. 2005. "Hardwiring for Maximum Fundraising Return on Investment." In *Expanding the Role of Philanthropy in Health Care,* edited by W. C. McGinly and K. Renzetti, 61–85. San Francisco: Jossey-Bass.

Gregory, A. G., and D. Howard. 2009. "The Nonprofit Starvation Cycle." *Stanford Social Innovation Review* 7 (4): 49–53.

Grizzard and Association for Healthcare Philanthropy. 2007. "Health Institutions Fail to Connect with 'Grateful Patients' According to New Survey by AHP and Grizzard." *Business Wire.* Published July 30. www.businesswire.com/news/home/20070730005110/en/Health-Institutions-Fail-Connect-Grateful-Patients-Survey.

Hall, F. R. 2005. "The Fundraising CEO." In *Expanding the Role of Philanthropy in Health Care: New Directions for Philanthropic Fundraising* 49, edited by W. C. McGinly and K. Renzetti, 43–50. San Francisco: Jossey-Bass.

Hanlon, P. 2006. *Primal Branding: Creating Zealots for Your Company, Your Brand, Your Future.* New York: Free Press.

Healthcare Financial Management Association (HFMA). 2009. "Philanthropy: Will It Save Your Operating Budget?" Published June 29. www.ahp.org/publication andtools/News/IntheNews/AHPInNews_2009/Pages/hfma62909.aspx.

Henderson, S. 2003. "The Trustee's Role in Fund Raising." In *Hank Rosso's Achieving Excellence in Fundraising,* 2nd ed., edited by E. R. Tempel, 335–48. San Francisco: Jossey-Bass.

Hodson, J. B. 2010. "Leading the Way: The Role of Presidents and Academic Deans in Fundraising." In *New Directions for Higher Education* 149, edited by J. B. Hodson and B. W. Speck, 39–49. San Francisco: Jossey-Bass.

Holmes, R. J., Jr., and J. B. Hodson. 2010. "The Challenge of Funding Fundraising." In *New Directions for Higher Education* 149, edited by J. B. Hodson and B. W. Speck, 27–37. San Francisco: Jossey-Bass.

Independent Sector. 2002. "Giving and Volunteering in the United States, 2001: Findings from a National Survey." Accessed June 14. www.cpanda.org/pdfs/gv/GV01Report.pdf.

Jones, R. M. 2011. "Love Endures Even Cancer." *New York Times* video, 5:48. May 17. video.nytimes.com/video/2011/05/16/health/100000000821590/love-endures-all-even-cancer.html.

Kadet, A. 2010. "How Charities Get You to Give." *Smart Money.* Published November 30. www.smartmoney.com/spending/budgeting/how-charities-get-you-to-give/#ixzz1CCNov2aD.

Kelly, L. 2007. *Beyond Buzz: The Next Generation of Word-of-Mouth Marketing.* New York: AMACOM.

Kinard, J. W. 2011. Personal communication, September 12.

Kristof, N. D. 2007. "Save the Darfur Puppy." *New York Times.* Published May 10. www.nytimes.com/2007/05/10/opinion/10kristof.html.

Lammers, J. A. 2003. "Know Your Ratios? Everyone Else Does." *Nonprofit Quarterly* 10 (1): 34–39.

Larkin, M. 2011. Personal communication, September 15.

Levis, B. 1993. "ROI Analysis." *Philanthropy Monthly* (spring): 23–37. nccsdataweb .urban.org/PubApps/levis/roi.html.

Littlejohn, W. S. 2011. Personal communication, September 13.

Long, C. 2011. Personal communication, September 25.

Mather, C. 1816. *Essays to Do Good; Addressed to All Christians Whether in Public or Private Capacities.* London: Williams and Son.

McNally, J. 2010. "The More Victims, the Less Severe the Judgment." *Wired Science.* Published September 13. www.wired.com/wiredscience/2010/09/scope-severity-paradox.

Moody's Investors Service. 2010. "Not-for-Profit Healthcare Medians for Fiscal Year 2009 Show Improvement Across All Major Ratios and All Rating Categories." Published August 24. www.alacrastore.com/research/moodys-global-credit-research-Not_for_Profit_Healthcare_Medians_for_Fiscal_Year_2009_Show_Improvement_Across_All_Major_Ratios_and_All_Rating_Categories-PBM_PBM127141.

———. 2006. "Fundraising at Not-for-Profit Hospitals Largely Untapped but Increasing." Accessed May 4. www.alacrastore.com/research/moodys-global-credit-research-Fundraising_at_Not_for_Profit_Hospitals_Largely_Untapped_but_Increasing-PBM_PBM96988.

Murray, C. 2011. Personal communication, September 2.

Nicoson, D. J. 2010. "Prospect Development Systems: Empowering Artful Fundraising." In *New Directions for Higher Education: Perspectives on Fundraising* 149, edited by J. B. Hodson and B. W. Speck, 73–79. San Francisco: Jossey-Bass.

Nocera, K. 2011. "Health Care's 'Unicorn' Gets Real." *Politico*. Published March 11. www.politico.com/news/stories/0311/51063.html.

Nowicki, M. 2001. *The Financial Management of Hospitals and Healthcare Organizations*, 2nd ed. Chicago: Health Administration Press.

Page, L. 2011. "6 Ways Hospital CEOs Can Boost Donations to Their Institutions." *Becker's Hospital Review*. Published January 4. www.beckershospitalreview.com/hospital-management-administration/6-ways-hospital-ceos-can-boost-donations-to-their-institutions.html.

Panas, J. 2003. "Fundraising's Four Magic Questions." Accessed May 4. www2.guidestar.org/rxa/news/articles/2007/fundraisings-four-magic-questions-answer-these-and-the-gift-is-yours.aspx?articleId=1108.

Parker-Pope, T. 2008. "Doctor and Patient, Now at Odds." *New York Times*. Published July 29. www.nytimes.com/2008/07/29/health/29well.html.

Pascal Murray. 2012. Executive Vice President Job Description. Accessed May 4. www.paschalmurray.com/positions/JobDetail.cfm?jobid=290.

Penn Medicine. 2012. "The Story of the Creation of the Nation's First Hospital." Accessed May 4. www.uphs.upenn.edu/paharc/features/creation.html.

Peters, T. 2007. "What's Culture Got to Do with It?" Posted February 16. www.tompeters.com/dispatches/009550.php.

Philanthropy Leadership Council. 2005. "Champion for the Cause: Maximizing the CEO's Effectiveness in Advancing Philanthropy." Washington DC: Advisory Board Company. Accessed May 4. www.advisory.com/Research/Philanthropy-Leadership-Council/Studies/2005/Champion-for-the-Cause.

Picha, D. 2011. Personal communication, September 12.

Piliavin, I. M., J. A. Piliavin, and J. Rodin. 1975. "Costs of Diffusion and the Stigmatized Victim." *Journal of Personality and Social Psychology* 32: 429–39.

Propp, V. 1928. *Morfologija Skazki (Morphology of the Folktale)*. Leningrad.

Random House. 2005. *Random House Webster's Unabridged Dictionary*, 2nd ed. New York: Random House Reference.

Ritchhart, R. 2000. "Of Dispositions, Attitudes, and Habits: Exploring How Emotions Shape Our Thinking." In *Harvard Project Zero*. Accessed May 4. learnweb.harvard.edu/alps/thinking/docs/article1.html.

Rooney, P. M., and S. K. Nathan. 2011. "Contemporary Dynamics of Philanthropy." In *Achieving Excellence in Fundraising*, 3rd ed., edited by E. R. Tempel, E. L. Seiler, and E. E. Aldrich, 117–24. San Francisco: John Wiley & Sons.

Russ Reid. 2010. *Heart of the Donor*. www.heartofthedonor.com.

Sargeant, A., and J. Shang. 2010. *Fundraising Principles and Practice*. San Francisco: Jossey-Bass.

Schein, E. H. 2010. *Organizational Culture and Leadership*, 3rd ed. San Francisco: Jossey-Bass.

Schwartz, C., J. B. Meisenhelder, M. Yunsheng, and G. Reed. 2003. "Altruistic Social Interest Behaviors Are Associated with Better Mental Health." *Psychosomatic Medicine* 65 (5): 778–85.

Seaver, R. E., 2011. Personal communication, October 1.

Shinkman, R. 2010. "Non-Profit Hospitals Improve Margins—For Now." *Fierce Health Finance*. Published September 1. www.fiercehealthfinance.com/story/non-profit-hospitals-improve-margins-now/2010-09-01.

Sikes, S. H. 2011. Personal communication, September 9.

Small, D. A., G. Loewenstein, and P. Slovic. 2004. "Can Insight Breed Callousness? The Impact of Learning About the Identifiable Victim Effect on Sympathy." *Decision Research Report* No. 04-01.

Stanley, T. J., and W. D. Danko. 1996. *The Millionaire Next Door*. Atlanta, GA: Longstreet Press.

Tempel, E. 2003. "Contemporary Dynamics of Philanthropy." In *Achieving Excellence in Fundraising*, 2nd ed., edited by E. Tempel, 3–13. San Francisco: John Wiley & Sons.

W. K. Kellogg Foundation. 2004. "Kellogg Logic Model Development Guide." Accessed May 4. www.wkkf.org/knowledge-center/resources/2006/02/WK-Kellogg-Foundation-Logic-Model-Development-Guide.aspx.

Index

About the Author

Betsy Chapin Taylor has worked in healthcare philanthropy for 17 years, serving as chief development officer and foundation president for academic, community, public, and faith-based healthcare systems. She is a principal consultant with Third Sector Strategy, specializing in fund development, board relations, and communications. She also has experience in healthcare marketing, political advance work, and journalism.

Taylor has an MS in journalism from Columbia University in New York and an MBA from the University of Georgia. In addition, she is an accredited Fellow of the Association for Healthcare Philanthropy (the highest level of certification for healthcare fund development professionals) and a member of the American College of Healthcare Executives.

Taylor is a frequent presenter on healthcare philanthropy for the American College of Healthcare Executives, the Association for Healthcare Philanthropy, the Children's Hospital Association, and other nonprofit and healthcare organizations.